D1385068

The Economy of China

The History and Culture of China

Mason Crest Publishers   Philadelphia

Shu Shin Luh

Ancient History of China

Art and Architecture of China

China Under Reform

The Economy of China

Famous People of China

Food and Festivals of China

The Geography of China

The Government of China

The History of Modern China

The People of China

The Economy of China

The History and Culture of China

Mason Crest Publishers Philadelphia

Shu Shin Luh

Produced by OTTN Publishing, Stockton, New Jersey

Mason Crest Publishers
370 Reed Road
Broomall, PA 19008
www.masoncrest.com

Printed and bound in India.

First printing

1 3 5 7 9 8 6 4 2

Library of Congress Cataloging-in-Publication Data

Luh, Shu Shin.
The economy of China / Shu Shin Luh.
p. cm. — (China)
Includes bibliographical references and index.
ISBN 1-59084-825-X
1. China—Economic conditions. 2. China—Economic policy. I. Title.
II. China (Broomall, Pa.).
HC427.L613 2004
330.951—dc22

2004011641

Table of Contents

Introduction

Dr. Jianwei Wang
University of Wisconsin–Stevens Point

Before his first official visit to the United States in December 2003, Chinese premier Wen Jiabao granted a lengthy interview to the *Washington Post.* In that interview, he observed: "If I can speak very honestly and in a straightforward manner, I would say the understanding of China by some Americans is not as good as the Chinese people's understanding of the United States." Needless to say, Mr. Wen is making a sweeping generalization here. From my personal experience and observation, some Americans understand China at least as well as some Chinese understand the United States. But overall there is some truth in Mr. Wen's remarks. For example, if you visited a typical high school in China, you would probably find that students there know more about the United States than their American counterparts know about China. For one thing, most Chinese teenagers start learning English in high school, while only a very small fraction of American high school students will learn Chinese.

In a sense, the knowledge gap between Americans and Chinese about each other is understandable. For the

Chinese, the United States is the most important foreign country, representing not just the most developed economy, unrivaled military might, and the most advanced science and technology, but also a very attractive political and value system, which many Chinese admire. But for Americans, China is merely one of many foreign countries. As citizens of the world's sole superpower, Americans naturally feel less compelled to learn from others. The Communist nature of the Chinese polity also gives many Americans pause. This gap of interest in and motivation to learn about the other side could be easily detected by the mere fact that every year tens of thousands of Chinese young men and women apply for a visa to study in the United States. Many of them decide to stay in this country. In comparison, many fewer Americans want to study in China, let alone live in that remote land.

Nevertheless, for better or worse, China is becoming more and more important to the United States, not just politically and economically, but also culturally. Most notably, the size of the Chinese population in the United States has increased steadily. China-made goods as well as Chinese food have become a part of most Americans' daily life. China is now the third-largest trade partner of the United States and will be a huge market for American goods and services. China is also one of the largest creditors, with about $100 billion in U.S. government securities. Internationally China could either help or hinder American foreign policy in the United Nations, on issues ranging from North Korea to non-proliferation of weapons of mass destruction. In the last century, misperception of this vast country cost the United States dearly in the Korean War and the Vietnam War. On the issue of Taiwan, China and the United States may once again embark on a collision course if both sides are not careful in handling the dispute. Simply put, the state of U.S.-China relations may well shape the future not just for Americans and Chinese, but for the world at large as well.

The main purpose of this series, therefore, is to help high school students form an accurate, comprehensive, and balanced understanding of China, past and present, good and bad, success and failure, potential and limit, and culture and state. At least three major images will emerge from various volumes in this series.

First is the image of traditional China. China has the longest continuous civilization in the world. Thousands of years of history produced a rich and sophisticated cultural heritage that still influences today's China. While this ancient civilization is admired and appreciated by many Chinese as well as foreigners, it can also be heavy baggage that makes progress in China difficult and often very costly. This could partially explain why China, once the most advanced country in the world, fell behind during modern times. Foreign encroachment and domestic trouble often plunged this ancient nation into turmoil and war. National rejuvenation and restoration of the historical greatness is still considered the most important mission for the Chinese people today.

Second is the image of Mao's China. The establishment of the People's Republic of China in 1949 marked a new era in this war-torn land. Initially the Communist regime was quite popular and achieved significant accomplishments by bringing order and stability back to Chinese society. When Mao declared that the "Chinese people stood up" at Tiananmen Square, "the sick man of East Asia" indeed reemerged on the world stage as a united and independent power. Unfortunately, Mao soon plunged the country into endless political campaigns that climaxed in the disastrous Cultural Revolution. China slipped further into political suppression, diplomatic isolation, economic backwardness, and cultural stagnation.

Third is the image of China under reform. Mao's era came to an abrupt end after his death in 1976. Guided by Deng Xiaoping's farsighted and courageous policy of reform and openness, China has experienced earth-shaking changes in the last quarter century. With the adoption of a market economy, China has transformed itself into a global economic powerhouse in only two decades. China has also become a full-fledged member of the international community, as exemplified by its return to the United Nations and its accession to the World Trade Organization. Although China is far from being democratic as measured by Western standards, overall it is now a more humane place to live, and the Chinese people have begun to enjoy unprecedented freedom in a wide range of social domains.

These three images of China, strikingly different, are closely related with one another. A more sophisticated and balanced perception of China needs to take into consideration all three images and the process of their evolution from one to another, thus acknowledging the great progress China has made while being fully aware that it still has a long way to go. In my daily contact with Americans, I quite often find that their views of China are based on the image of traditional China and of China under Mao—they either discount or are unaware of the dramatic changes that have taken place. Hopefully this series will allow its readers to observe the following realities about China.

First, China is not black and white, but rather—like the United States—complex and full of contradictions. For such a vast country, one or two negative stories in the media often do not represent the whole picture. Surely the economic reforms have reduced many old problems, but they have also created many new problems. Not all of these problems, however, necessarily prove the guilt of the Communist system. Rather, they may be the result of the very reforms the government has been implementing and of the painful transition from one system to another. Those who would view China through a single lens will never fully grasp the complexity of that country.

Second, China is not static. Changes are taking place in China every day. Anyone who lived through Mao's period can attest to how big the changes have been. Every time I return to China, I discover something new. Some things have changed for the better, others for the worse. The point I want to make is that today's China is a very dynamic society. But the development in China has its own pace and logic. The momentum of changes comes largely from within rather than from without. Americans can facilitate but not dictate such changes.

Third, China is neither a paradise nor a hell. Economically China is still a developing country with a very low per capita GDP because of its huge population. As the Chinese premier put it, China may take another 100 years to catch up with the United States. China's political system remains authoritarian and can be repressive and arbitrary. Chinese people still do not have as much freedom as American people enjoy, particularly when it comes to expressing opposition to the government. So China is certainly not an ideal society, as its leaders used to believe (or at least declare). Yet the Chinese people as a whole are much better off today than they were 20 years ago, both economically and politically. Chinese authorities were fond of telling the Chinese people that Americans lived in an abyss of misery. Now every Chinese knows that this is nonsense. It is equally ridiculous to think of the Chinese in a similar way.

Finally, China is both different from and similar to the United States. It is true that the two countries differ greatly in terms of political and social systems and cultural tradition. But it is also true that China's program of reform and openness has made these two societies much more similar. China is largely imitating the United States in many aspects. One can easily detect the convergence of the two societies in terms of popular culture, values, and lifestyle by walking on the streets of Chinese cities like Shanghai. With ever-growing economic and other functional interactions, the two countries have also become increasingly interdependent. That said, it is naïve to expect that China will become another United States. Even if China becomes a democracy one day, these two great nations may still not see eye to eye on many issues.

Understanding an ancient civilization and a gigantic country such as China is always a challenge. If this series kindles readers' interest in China and provides them with systematic information and thoughtful perspectives, thus assisting their formation of an informed and realistic image of this fascinating country, I am sure the authors of this series will feel much rewarded.

The skyline of Shanghai, modern China's commercial capital. By the early 21st century, China had emerged as a powerful force in the world economy.

Overview

From atop the Jin Mao Building, Shanghai's tallest skyscraper, the view tells an extraordinary story. It is the story of a city's remarkable development—of how, in a mere decade of frenzied building, some 3,000 high-rises went up and acres of rice paddies were transformed into a steel, glass, and concrete world of ultramodern office towers, five-star hotels, and glittering shopping malls. The sheer volume of construction was so great that some parts of Shanghai have begun to sink in the area's soft soil. What would China's revolutionary leader, Mao Zedong, think if he saw today's Shanghai, China's commercial capital, blazing with neon lights, its streets bustling with traffic and its port filled with ships from all over the world?

Of course, if Mao were to return, he would have more than the bustle of Shanghai to ponder. The forces that transformed Shanghai into a mecca of capitalism are playing out elsewhere in China. Mayors of Chinese cities woo foreign companies with tax breaks and other incentives to attract investment. And farmers, once the backbone of China's economy, take a backseat now to the new drivers of economic development: the entrepreneurs who make millions selling low-cost, sophisticated computer chips and flat-screen televisions made in China to the rest of the world. Today's China is the third-largest importer in the world, just behind Germany and the United States. It is also the world's largest producer of televisions and makes a quarter of the world's washing machines and half of the world's cameras and photocopiers. China is one of the world's largest oil markets, trailing behind only Japan and the United States. While China remains at its core a developing nation ruled by one party—the Chinese Communist Party—the country today holds little resemblance to the China that Mao built on the shoulders of poor and uneducated farmers.

Looking at China from the outside, it has often been easy to judge the "Middle Kingdom" by its tragic layers of history—the tens of thousands who died building the Great Wall, the chaos of the Cultural Revolution, and more recently the shocking massacre at Tiananmen Square. For decades, the People's Republic of China was seen as a nation isolated from the rest of the world, torn internally by political struggles and haunted by its imperial past. The Chinese Communist Party, which came to power after World War II, grounded itself in the age-old ideology of a state-centric society, basing governance entirely on the influence and decisions of the state. This meant strong personal leadership at the apex, and impressive nationwide governing bureaucracies. The message was simple: The people need not worry; the government will take care of everything. Under this system, many scholars say, the kind of investment behavior and technological change necessary for healthy, modern economic growth was stymied.

And as a result, too many foreigners were quick to dismiss the potential of this sleeping giant called China.

No longer. Today, a whole new generation of Chinese politicians, entrepreneurs, and thinkers has come of age, relatively untouched by the nation's painful past. Financial reforms put in place in the 1970s after Mao's death are finally making an impact. The rapid economic liberalization—opening the country to foreign investment, trade, and industrialization—has created a version of Chinese capitalism that has generated unprecedented economic prosperity for the country. In the early years of the 21st century, when the global economy was suffering a slump, China boasted annual growth rates in its gross domestic product of 8 percent. The sleeping giant, as one prominent economist put it, has awakened, and the rest of the world can no longer ignore its presence and its potential.

A New Revolution

How did this transformation come about? External influences, from U.S. president Richard Nixon's landmark visit to China in 1972 to the Asian financial crisis of the mid-1990s, played a role. In particular, the financial crisis that hit Southeast Asian nations such as Indonesia, Malaysia, Thailand, and the Philippines exposed the weaknesses in those economies, leaving them in shambles. But it also opened a window of opportunity for China to step up its influence in Asia. To take advantage of this new opening, China's centralized state system had to change. The ruling Chinese Communist Party had to relinquish some of its tight grip over the country. Therefore, the more significant part of China's economic evolution came from within. The Chinese Communist Party, which once reviled businessmen as corrupt "capitalist roaders" is now embracing them as benefactors of China's economic boom. The government is luring overseas Chinese to return home

President Richard M. Nixon and his wife, Pat, pose on the Great Wall of China. Nixon's historic 1972 visit opened the way for warmer relations, and trade ties, between the United States and China.

with glossy pamphlets about the high quality of life in major Chinese cities. It is tempting homegrown businessmen to be more proactive and innovative by offering them tax breaks. And it is showing these business moguls the Communist Party matters by offering them influential positions within the Party.

Today, the people of China see their country's growing economic and political influence as a new revolution, one that is transforming the nation and elevating it to a new international level. Yesterday's factory workers can be today's entrepreneurs, fashioning a neon dreamscape from ancient alleyways. Overseas Chinese return from five years abroad to find their hometowns unrecognizable, while in the interior, whole new cities are sprouting out of rice paddies. Designers are fashioning a new Chinese aesthetic, blending the now with the then. Business moguls are building economic empires, flooding Asia with their cutting-edge products. Even the Chinese Communist Party is trying to reinvent itself by inviting once-disdained capitalists into its fold.

Global Ramifications

For China's neighbors and its trading partners, the flourishing Chinese economy is both a blessing and a threat. On the one hand, an open-door China means access to the country's more than 1.2 billion consumers. According to the latest data from the World

Bank, an international lending and development group, China ranks as one of the top importers of foreign goods. Well-known multinational companies such as McDonald's, Coca-Cola, and Procter & Gamble recognize this: U.S. multinationals have together invested well over $3 billion to establish their presence in the country. Some economists predict that in the next 15 to 20 years, China's economy has the potential to be as big as the U.S. economy is today. If that prediction holds true, there will be beneficiaries in the rest of the world as well.

Still, there remains a real fear among China's trading partners, and understandably so, that China's rapid growth could mean bad news for their own economies. China, Hong Kong included, accounts for close to 70 percent of all foreign investments in Asia, and that percentage is likely to increase now that China has joined the World Trade Organization, the highest regulatory body for international trade. There are real fears that investments being drawn into China will accelerate, very possibly marginalizing economies in the rest of the region, and even some sectors of the developed world. The reality is also this: most economies, both developing and developed, cannot compete with China's vast pool of cheap, skilled and semi-skilled labor and its immense market. China's eastern seaboard alone is home to an urban middle class numbering 400 million to 500 million, with an appetite and ability to pay for everything from mobile phones to computers.

So is China a friend or a rival? That is the question many governments, corporations, and scholars are asking, and while the answer may vary slightly depending on who is asked, for now, there is a broad consensus that an economically strong China is more or less good for the global economy. Take the United States, for example. China's growth has certainly put a strain on the U.S. economy, but it has also brought benefits. On the one hand, the United States runs a large trade deficit with China—the deficit stood at $103

A worker unloads boxes of Coca-Cola soft drinks from a delivery truck outside a restaurant in Beijing. Today, many multinational corporations are working to establish their brands in the world's most populous country.

billion in 2002, according to U.S. Commerce Department statistics. This means, in the simplest terms, that as a whole, the United States imports more goods from China than it is able to export to the country. That said, however, within the overall trade deficit, the United States runs surpluses in certain areas. For example, the United States enjoyed a surplus of $1.1 billion in agricultural trade with China in 2002, and that surplus was projected to rise to $3.5 billion in 2003. The United States also runs surpluses in the services trade; the figure stood at just under $2 billion in 2002.

A similar situation prevails among many of China's Southeast Asian neighbors. China's rapid economic liberalization, especially after its entry into the World Trade Organization in 2001, has meant a noticeable redirection of foreign investments into China instead of Southeast Asian countries, many of which badly need the money to rebuild their battered economies. Even so, free trade agreements with China have given Southeast Asia's homegrown corporations better access to the huge Chinese consumer market through lower tariff rates (taxes for importing goods to a foreign country) and the exchange of technology know-how.

Any which way the analysis goes, it is obvious that those that enter China's economic orbit will prosper. Those that cannot—or will not—are likely to suffer and decline, and this applies to both the developed and developing economies of the world. China's massive population and its ability to offer both skilled and unskilled labor to satisfy the whole range of industries—from low-end manufacturing to sophisticated computer chip production—will continue to pressure its trading partners. But the so-called China threat is perhaps only an exaggerated perspective. China is still a relative newcomer to the world trade arena, and it has much work ahead to truly liberalize its economy. At the market level, China will need better commercial laws to protect intellectual property rights and hold corporations to minimum ethical standards, among other concerns. Beyond market access, China will have to make some difficult internal adjustments, such as reformulating many of its economic policies to bring them in line with international standards, strengthening social safety nets, and narrowing the economic and social disparities among regions within the country.

This much is certain: China is now an important part of the global economy, a country with a vast pool of labor and resources that cannot be ignored. It is essential that we begin to understand how this awakening giant is structured and what oils its economic engines.

Mao Zedong votes in a local election, 1953. As leader of the People's Republic of China between 1949 and 1976, Mao wielded a great deal of influence in economic matters—often with disastrous results.

2 A Historical Look at China's Economy

Close to a century ago, in the Hunan Provincial Library in southeastern China, a 19-year-old farm boy looked for the first time in his life at a map of the world. He studied it, as he later recalled, with great interest. He probably could not have imagined, though, that someday he would be redrawing the world map with an iron pen dipped in red ink. In 1949, much to the shock of the Western world, Mao Zedong, the founding father of the People's Republic of China, added his country of half a billion to the domain of world communism.

For the West—and especially the United States, which had fallen into a tense ideological struggle with the Soviet Union—this appeared to be a disaster of the first magnitude, as the world's most populous nation had joined the ranks of its Cold War adversary. For the

Soviets and other advocates of communism, it constituted the greatest victory since the Russian Revolution of 1917 and seemed to augur the inevitable triumph of the proletariat (laboring classes), as Karl Marx had confidently predicted the previous century. For most of the Chinese people, the global ramifications were less important than the fact that their country was finally at peace, after more than four decades of intermittent factional fighting and the war with Japan. As it turned out, peace would unfortunately not mean an end to widespread discord or massive suffering within China.

When Mao, the peasant boy–turned–world leader, pronounced China a domain of communism in 1949, he became master over the vast land that had bred him, over the cities and the villages, the farmlands and the rivers—and over half a billion tough, tired people who were looking to him for hope and prosperity. He intended to deliver by radically transforming Chinese society, steeped as it was in thousands of years of tradition. By the time Mao died in 1976, he had transformed his country—but not necessarily all in ways that benefited the Chinese people. His economic policies were erratic and frequently ill-conceived; his insistence on ideological conformity was unyielding; and, particularly in his later years, his suspicion of, and jealousy toward, political rivals verged on paranoia. The result was a roller-coaster ride of political purges, recurring social chaos, and a drained economy. Ultimately Mao was responsible, directly or indirectly, for the deaths of millions of Chinese people during his nearly three decades of rule.

Mao successors, some of whom he had trained—and some, like Deng Xiaoping, whom he had also at one time purged—spent much of the late 1970s and beyond attempting to reverse his policies, even as they claimed to revere them. Mao had withdrawn China into isolationism, even from the Soviet Union, its Communist neighbor and early benefactor; his successors would open the doors to global economics. The post-Mao leaders would also return to the Chinese people the opportunities to express their entrepreneurial skills, leading to astonishing rates of growth as well as a complete transformation of the face of China's cities. Still, despite the agony Mao caused, the changes and moves toward a new flexibility that came after his death must be considered in the context of his legacy. Even as Mao's allegiance lay with the farmers whom he galvanized to consolidate his power, he was also deeply responsible for creating policy in the mid-20th century that set in motion the beginnings of China's shift from a predominantly agricultural society to the industrializing nation that it is today.

China's Economy Before the Second World War

The evolution of the Chinese economy cannot be understood in isolation from the political ups and downs that characterized 20th-century Chinese history. The turn of that century marked for China the end of thousands of years of imperial rule. The last emperor of the Qing dynasty, Pu-yi, abdicated in February 1912. But what followed was hardly a smooth transition from the imperial dynasties to a republic. There were power struggles among those who had helped overthrow the emperor. There were debates about how to build a republican state that would close the economic gap between the rich and the poor. And, in many areas of the country, the national government exercised little or no authority, as warlords maintained actual control.

Any hope in the early 20th century to establish a new republic in place of the antiquated imperial system disappeared when Sung Chiao-jen, the leader of a major political party, was assassinated. In the midst of this chaos, the nucleus of the Chinese Communist Party (CCP) established itself. The CCP's four major priorities were national reunification, organization of the urban proletariat for socialist revolution, redress of the terrible poverty and exploitation in China's countryside, and eradication of the forces of foreign imperialism (since the mid-1800s various nations had been infringing on Chinese national sovereignty). Those callings resonated with the disenfranchised and the forgotten—the farmers, the people living in rural areas, and the urban working class—who saw the ruling Nationalist Party demonstrating a level of corruption on par with the old imperial system.

In spite of the political unrest that followed the overthrow of the Qing dynasty, the economy developed steadily in the 25 years between 1912 and 1937. The energy and resourcefulness of the Chinese people, and their desire to make a better living, were sufficient to improve the economy once they were given some freedom to do so. During this time, a strong Chinese middle class began to emerge, particularly in major cities such as Shanghai and Guangzhou. In short, modernization was taking place.

In post-imperial China, beginning in 1912, the economy largely functioned as many economies around the world do today: as a market-based economy. Merchants exchanged goods freely without the government setting down stringent rules on what and how much could be traded, on who could trade, or on other regulatory matters. But robust trade was largely concentrated along the coast, in port cities such as Shanghai; much of the rest of China lacked the political stability necessary for strong commerce.

The larger cities were experiencing a notable growth in industry, but the benefits of that growth were distributed very unevenly. Workers in shipyards, railway machine shops, electrical plants, silk-weaving mills, thermos-bottle manufacturing plants, and copper-sheet factories, for example, might make the equivalent of approximately $30 per month, or in certain cases even more. (All dollar figures in this book refer to U.S. dollars.) But monthly wages in most other industries were far lower, falling to about $6 or below in the manufacturing plants for lime, dyes, neon lights, cement, acid, starch, alcohol, cotton waste, batteries, and matches. Wages for women and children were lower still: a woman working in the match industry or a child in a cotton mill would be lucky to bring home more than $2 or $3 a month. And hours for Chinese workers were long. During the 1920s, the shortest average workday recorded in any Chinese city was 9.5 hours, in Shanghai; in some provincial industrial centers, the workday averaged 12 or 13 hours.

Labor conditions in rural areas during this period were almost as bleak. The shift to a market-based economy in the early 20th century brought new types of pressures on rural areas, wrecking the rural handicraft and other sideline industries that kept peasant families above the poverty level. Much of the problem was also bound in exploitative land-tenure systems, abuses by moneylenders, and primitive agricultural technology that perpetuated the poverty of many in the rural farming communities. Tens of millions of farmers

For thousands of years peasant farmers formed the backbone of China's economy. But because of the small size of the typical Chinese farm plot, an exploitative feudal system, and other factors, the line between survival and starvation was razor thin for many farm families.

Weavers work on embroidered fabric in a factory in Shanshui. The development of small factories throughout China in the early years of the 20th century brought decidedly uneven benefits to Chinese workers.

owned farms that were too small to be fully viable economically. These peasants "overemployed" the labor of their family members on their farms, while to earn extra cash they hired out their own labor at the busiest times of the farm year, even though that was when they were most needed on their own land. Still, many more had to sell their children or watch them slowly starve.

With so many poverty-stricken laborers available, few of the wealthier farmers went to the expense of mechanizing the farm work, even when machinery and fuel were available. Nor did they invest much in draft animals such as water buffalos and donkeys, since the daily wages paid to a hired laborer were the same as the cost of a day's fodder for a single donkey. The man could be laid off when the need for him was over, but the donkey had to be fed and sheltered for the whole year, even when it was not being used.

The ruling Nationalist Party during the early 1900s did little to alleviate conditions for China's poor. The Japanese invasion in the late 1930s, and the continued fighting through the World War II years, further eroded its base of support. When the Japanese surrendered in 1945, the Chinese people were demoralized by the long years of fighting, and the Nationalist government, weakened by factional conflicts and the serious inflation that affected the areas under its control, was unable to reestablish its authority over areas formerly held by the Japanese. The Nationalist government also lacked the trained personnel to fill vacant positions, and without the money to rebuild China's war-shattered society, it began to lose its grip on power. The Communists, though they also lacked resources, were able to secure support at the grassroots level, and they attracted some of China's intellectuals, students, and urban workers to join their ranks as these groups became disillusioned with the Nationalists' ineptness and corruption.

China's Economy After 1949

For the Chinese Communists, reestablishing order would involve various difficult tasks: completely restructuring the bureaucracy and the governmental system; integrating the Chinese Communist Party into that system; curbing inflation; imposing basic land reform; and rooting out domestic opposition. These tasks were vastly complicated by the Korean War, to which China contributed massively between 1950 and 1953, and in which it suffered enormous casualties.

Once the war was over, Chinese leaders worked to complete the first stage of their strategy for economic growth. They formulated a comprehensive Five-Year Plan consciously based on the earlier experiences of the Soviet Union. In the Soviet Union, state-controlled industrial production in a sequence of detailed five-year programs was believed to have been responsible for the nation's emergence as a world-class power in the 1930s, with the ability to withstand and repulse the full force of Germany's attack in World War II. That victory, in turn, allowed the Soviet Union to expand greatly its influence in Europe at war's end, despite containment efforts by the United States. China's choice to adopt the Soviet model was certainly one way of emphasizing the anti-capitalist and anti-imperialist nature of the new Chinese state. The Chinese Communist Party, having seized power in a violent civil war, needed a framework for exercising its

U.S. Marines take cover behind a tank that is firing on Communist troops during the Korean War, May 1951. China's involvement in the conflict, which lasted from 1950 to 1953, severely limited the country's opportunities for economic development.

newly acquired power as it set out to build socialism in the poverty-stricken country.

To prepare for the task of economic restructuring, China's leaders set standards for bureaucratic recruitment and pay scales, introduced regular administrative procedures, and organized the people of China according to the local units in which they worked so as to increase the efficiency of social control and indoctrination. To heighten agricultural production and to prevent the reemergence of old, oppressive social patterns in the countryside, the government launched a radical wave of land reform that organized peasants into large-scale cooperatives of around 200 to 300 households each. Almost all of China's peasants were enrolled in these cooperatives by the end of 1956, and Mao's vision of a truly socialist China seemed to have taken a major step forward.

Political and Economic Missteps

Overlapping with the great shifts on the land was a political consolidation of Mao's power, and the establishment of policies that would eventually undermine his advocacy for the peasants. In part to win the support of China's students and intellectuals, Mao solicited criticism of the Communist Party and state programs—a level of free expression that the Party had not previously tolerated. For a few heady weeks in mid-1957, a torrent of criticism flowed in what was dubbed the Hundred Flowers Movement. Ultimately, though, Mao and the Communist Party proved unwilling to allow Chinese citizens to express their disapproval of the government, notwithstanding the fact that it was the Party chairman himself who had called for the criticism in the first place. The Party responded with a ruthless crackdown, labeling critics rightists and traitors to the Communist proletariat movement. Hundreds of thousands were imprisoned or otherwise punished.

A 1957 Chinese poster celebrating the country's economic development. The illustrations include Mao Zedong addressing a large crowd; views of a manufacturing plant, textiles in stores, girls doing needlework, and a girl using a microscope in a laboratory; a map showing the locations of Chinese industries; and charts tracking economic growth.

Now Mao and his fellow senior Communist Party leaders were at a crossroads. The country was under control politically and the economy was growing steadily, but the explosive growth in the countryside that had been hoped for had not materialized. The results of the First Five-Year Plan, which ended in 1955, were not ideal. In agriculture, production figures showed disappointingly small gains. Grain production, for example, increased only 1 percent in 1955, in the face of a 2 percent population rise. Cotton-cloth rations had to be cut because of shortages. Although the First Five-Year Plan had met its quotas, it had revealed disturbing imbalances in the Chinese economic system. While industrial output rose at about 18.7 percent per year during the plan period, agricultural production rose only about 3.8 percent.

Mao's response to the disappointing progress in agriculture was a new strategy of heightened production through moral incentives and mass mobilization under the direction of inspirational local Party leaders. By decentralizing economic decision making, this strategy would lead to even greater Party power in the countryside, and to a corresponding decline in the influence of professional economic planners. In Mao's mind, China's economic woes could be solved by the spontaneous energizing of the whole nation.

Mao did not actually understand economics, but he was extremely skillful in mobilizing the masses. He thought economic objectives could be achieved in the same way as political objectives and revolutions, simply by rallying mass support. In a wild and stirring campaign starting in 1958, farmers were organized into immense communes. (In the previous few years, they had been organized successively into "cooperatives.") The Great Leap Forward, as this economic program was optimistically labeled, was launched with a very noble goal in mind: inspiring human life and economy alike by ending all the old distinctions of gender, age, skill, and occupation. In the communes, people worked as a team and ate together in mess halls.

Industrial output was also to be rapidly increased. People were asked to build furnaces in their backyards to produce iron and steel. To satisfy the ambitious output targets for these metals, finished products such as pots and bicycles were melted down in the furnaces—a thoroughly irrational exercise. And ultimately much of the iron and steel produced was unusable because of its poor quality.

Mao hoped that the Great Leap Forward would make China an economic superpower. What resulted instead was an economic and human disaster unsurpassed in history. Mismanagement of the huge agricultural communes, combined with extended bad weather, caused food production to plummet. But commune managers, whose advancement in the Party was linked to their ability to meet or exceed production quotas, frequently exaggerated the actual harvests. As a result, grain sent to the central government from phony surpluses left people on the communes without enough to eat, and widespread starvation ensued. From 1958 to 1962, an estimated 25 million people died in the most severe famine in Chinese history.

Shaken to its roots, the Party sought to reorganize itself, reassert central control, and return the economy to a more predictable track. As in the period of the First Five-Year Plan, the careful orchestrations of comprehensive state planning came to the fore, and China's heavy industry, especially, was returned to a path of rapid and conventional growth. With Mao having largely retreated to the sidelines, a more moderate government started to allow peasants to farm on private plots of land, while the commune system still existed nominally. Unreasonable output targets were also abolished. In December 1964, Premier Zhou Enlai, essentially the third-in-command at the Chinese Communist Party, announced the government's objective to achieve "Four Modernizations" in China. The four areas were industry, agriculture, defense, and science and technology.

All this hopeful regeneration was nipped in the bud, however. In 1966 Chairman Mao and his closest supporters launched the Great

Young marchers carry banners and a large portrait of Chairman Mao during the Cultural Revolution, 1968. Economic stagnation accompanied the extreme social chaos that the Cultural Revolution visited upon China between 1966 and 1976.

Proletarian Cultural Revolution, an immense upheaval that would sputter along for a decade. It began innocently enough, with a 1965 literary controversy over a dramatic production staged by the Beijing Opera Troupe. The following May, Mao touched off the firestorm that would engulf all spheres of Chinese life—cultural as well as political, social, educational, and economic—by assailing "representatives of our party, our government, our armed forces and various cultural groups" as "a batch of counterrevolutionary revisionists" who would "try to seize power, turning the dictatorship of the proletariat into one of the capitalist class." Students in particular responded, and Mao and his supporters tapped the anger and revolutionary fervor of these youthful "Red Guards," turning them against their elders.

The Party bureaucracy was challenged as never before, and those who were not ousted were regrouped into "revolutionary committees" that allegedly instilled the new spirit of radicalism into every factory, commune, school, and work unit. Political power was transferred from the pragmatic economic planners to the radical elements of the Party, organized around the Red Guard (mainly teenagers and youth in their twenties)—often in the name of destroying an old cultural tradition that supposedly hindered the social revolution. China's educational system ceased to function, and universities closed. The ensuing political turmoil, including worker demands for higher wages, led to a resolution to freeze all prices at the end of 1966. Over the next 10 years, millions of "intellectuals" and "closet capitalists" were forced into manual labor, and tens of thousands of Chinese people were murdered by rampaging Red Guards, executed by the state, or killed in factional fighting. In addition to its human costs, the Cultural Revolution rendered impossible a properly functioning economy.

Scholars have tried to make sense of why Mao decided to dismantle the very establishment—the Chinese Communist Party—

that he had helped build. Some believe that the Cultural Revolution was born primarily of the chairman's megalomania. Mao, these observers feel, simply wanted to eliminate his political rivals and consolidate his power once again. Others believe that his motives had more to do with ideology (specifically, his conviction that revolution must be an ongoing process), or his recognition that the revolution had strayed from its original mission of uplifting the peasants and had merely replaced one exploitative ruling elite (the Nationalists) with another (the Communist Party bureaucracy).

A Change of Course

Whatever Mao's motivations in launching the Cultural Revolution, the result was another disaster. Chaos reigned for a decade, and the Chinese economy stagnated.

It was only after Mao's death in 1976 that reform-minded leaders finally had an opening to refocus China's economy toward achieving the goals of the Four Modernizations campaign, which had been cut short by the Cultural Revolution. Deng Xiaoping, who ascended to power in 1978, is given much of the credit for putting China on the path to recovery after a decade of dysfunction. Deng sought to reinvigorate Party members and to improve rural production, industrial management, foreign trade and investment, and science and technology. He toured the United States, demonstrating to the Western world his intentions to bring China back into the international arena. Soon 10,000 Chinese academic and technical specialists were studying in the United States, while 100,000 American tourists were taking their dollars to China each year.

Deng's policy of opening China acknowledged that the Chinese economy could progress only with a greater infusion of technology and capital, both obtained from abroad. Technology transfer became a major objective. Contracts with foreign firms for new machinery, factories, production processes, tourist hotels, and the extraction of coal and oil promised simultaneously to bring in both capital and technology.

In the following two decades, China would experience tremendous economic growth. The success of the reforms has been attributed to a variety of factors, including canny leadership from Chinese officials, especially Deng; a pragmatic approach to development; experimentation; support from the Party as well as the populace; and relative political stability.

When it entered the World Trade Organization in 2001, China agreed to open its markets to foreign agricultural producers—a development likely to create additional pressures for China's peasant farmers, many of whom continue to rely on traditional methods of cultivation.

3

Agriculture: The Engine for Modern China

Farmers have long been at the center of the Chinese economy. During the 19th and early 20th centuries, most Chinese were rural people. Most Chinese farmers owned some land and often had sources of income apart from farm work, such as handicrafts. Yet life was generally harsh. Farm plots were very small, averaging less than two acres per family, and peasants had little access to new technology, capital, or cheap transport.

Traditional Marxist thinking, from which communism largely derived its ideology, relegated peasants to a class that Marx believed represented "barbarism within civilization," people who were unable to develop revolutionary consciousness and only wanted land

and bread (food). During the Russian Revolution, Lenin revised Marx's view, assigning peasants a more supporting revolutionary role, though he still believed that it was the urban working class that initiated revolution.

Only in China would Communist thinkers truly elevate the role of the peasants. In the 1920s, for example, Chinese leftists began to change their view of the revolutionary potential of the rural population. Some, like the Nationalist Party organizers in southern China, had great success from 1921 to 1923 in convincing disaffected farmers to form peasant associations and challenge oppressive landlords. Likewise, Mao Zedong's own work in the rural areas in 1925 and 1926 led him to see the farmers differently. Mao recognized the plight of the oppressed peasantry, trapped for thousands of years by a rigid feudal system whereby they farmed the lands of the rich. It was clear to Mao early on that the peasants had to be the chief revolutionists. His belief in rural revolution thus became a hallmark of Chinese Communist thinking.

Peasants in the Early Years of the People's Republic

Soon after Mao's Chinese Communist Party consolidated its power, it moved quickly to organize the agricultural sector into collectives. In the Soviet Union during the early 1930s, the city cadres had entered the countryside to attack and destroy the rich peasantry, who fought back by destroying livestock, fomenting opposition, and generally refusing to go along. The Soviet collectivization had been immensely destructive. In China, however, the Chinese Communist Party from early on established itself as a rural organization, close to and dependent upon the rural villages for its power, and it knew how to take gradual steps toward its eventual goal.

The first stage was to organize the peasantry into mutual-aid teams, in which a half dozen or so households pooled their labor, tools, and animals and helped one another during the harvest season. The second stage was to set up agricultural producers' cooperatives, in which larger numbers of farm families (30 to 50 households) pooled not only their labor and equipment but also their land. Because the farmers got a return, or dividend, in proportion to the amount of land they contributed to the cooperative—and because they still held title to the land—this second step diminished resistance from the rich peasant community, whose position at first did not decline but actually improved.

The early 1950s would be remembered as a honeymoon period between the Chinese Communist Party and the rural peasantry. Growth in trade, sideline production, and education, along with small village mutual-aid teams and cooperatives, seemed to promise a better future. And at this point, while land had been shifted from the 2.6 percent of landlord households to former tenants and landless laborers,

Mao walks with a group of smiling peasants in this not-so-subtle Chinese illustration meant to evoke admiration for the chairman and support for his agricultural reforms of the 1950s.

During the 1950s, Chinese farmers were organized into progressively larger groups: mutual-aid teams consisting of a handful of families, cooperatives of 30 to 50 households, huge agricultural collectives. By the end of the decade, the commune system regulated and controlled virtually all facets of rural life—and productivity fell.

land could still be bought and sold privately. The result was a more contented peasant class—and one that was loath to give up the idea of private property, even if many peasants actually had rather meager landholdings.

Soon, however, came the third stage of the Chinese Communist Party's plan for the agricultural sector: collectivization. The agricultural producers' cooperatives were merged into larger units, and on these new collectives all peasants worked for wages only—regardless of their input of property, tools, animals, and land. Mao's impetuous demand for this further move was debated and initially resisted by many within the Chinese Communist Party, but local Party leaders generated more than enough zeal to force a total redistribution of landlord holdings and give the collectivization campaign true momentum. The goal of this stage, in Mao's mind, was to level the playing field for the poor peasants who had long been locked into the feudal system of farming other people's land and paying tenancy, which perpetuated their poverty.

In reality, the collectivization campaign simply led to the emergence of a new elite from the peasant society: the activists of the Chinese Communist Party who had helped organize the movement. This new peasant leadership was self-selected, as ambitious and energetic younger people found opportunity to rise in the new power structure. Intensely political in every act, this new elite instinctively sought status, power, and privileges that set them apart from the masses and entrenched them as the new local leadership. The nominal success in collectivization was hailed as a giant step toward economic benefit in the countryside. In fact, however, it was the final penetration of the state into the farm household, the politicization of peasant life in order to control it.

The Chinese Farmer, 1958–1978

During the 20 years from 1958 to 1978, most of the people in

This 1956 poster was designed to explain Chinese Communist Party plans for the development of agriculture over the following decade. Ultimately those plans went horribly awry, contributing to a massive famine that claimed millions of lives.

rural China would become locked in an umbilical relationship with the state. How the Party secured the grain supply to feed the growing cities became a basic story of the Maoist era.

The structure of agricultural collectivization was capped in 1958 by the establishment of communes. Once this structure was completed, the individual farmer found himself toiling under six levels of administration. Beneath China's 2,000 counties were 70,000 communes. Beneath these communes were 750,000 brigades, each of which was roughly the size of a village and had about 220 households, or almost 1,000 persons. Beneath the brigades were the 5 million production teams, each composed of about 33 households or 145 persons.

Villagers obtained their own grain rations by showing their certificates of household registration. These papers specified where they lived. If they traveled to another region, they could not secure rations there. Farmers under this system were basically fixed upon the land, dependent entirely for food on the production team in which they worked. The paradox was that the revolutionary state, having established its legitimacy by freeing the peasant from landlordism and other constraints, now had the peasant boxed in as never before. The state had become the ultimate landlord, and maintaining legitimacy in that role put statecraft to the test.

But the peasant was never made to feel cheated by the state. Mao was able to do this by keeping the agricultural tax at a minimum so that no one could claim the state was taking too much from the peasant. The state also established a level beyond which the harvest was considered a surplus and then asked each production team to contribute grain (mainly rice or wheat) from its "surplus" by selling it to the state at the state's low fixed price. Which team could contribute the most grain to Chairman Mao? In this endeavor peasants could feel as though they were benefactors, and not serfs.

The Realities of Farming Under Communism

Until the economic reforms that began in 1978 dismantled the commune farming system, agricultural production in China lagged behind hopes and expectations. Meanwhile, China's population was growing steadily. In 1953–1954 there were some 586 million Chinese. By 1957 that number had risen to an estimated 630 million; by 1970, to 820 million; and by 1974, to 880 million. China's population topped 1 billion by the early 1980s and had reached 1.2 billion by the end of the decade. This large increase in the number of people ate up any production gains to be had, and it strained the resources of space and housing as well as public services. Moreover, China's huge labor force was undertrained, and a quarter or more of the population was illiterate.

Despite the disparities between the rich and the poor, the literate and those who could not read or write, the skilled and the unskilled, under Mao's plan, everyone was equal, and everyone was guaranteed a job and a livelihood. But this also meant that the uneven abilities of the workers inhibited any improvements in productivity. In spite of (or because of) the heavy investment in industry, the rural standard of living stagnated.

The original strategy for agricultural development had assumed that China's labor force could itself provide the infrastructure of irrigation, roads, and fields, if it could be properly motivated. The establishment of cooperatives and rural communes in the 1950s did indeed make available a great deal of unused rural labor power. Although the labor invested in moving earth and cutting rock was at the time very expensive, it was argued that eventually there would be greater production and productivity per person. Unfortunately, this self-sufficient strategy in agriculture, although widely advocated for developing countries, seldom worked out. Improvements came from tube-well water pumps more than from irrigation channels, and from fertilizers, insecticides, and better strains of crop rather than from large, level fields.

During the Maoist era, agriculture actually saw a decline in productivity per worker-hour even though the labor invested and the product secured both increased. The entire three decades of Maoist agricultural management only perpetuated the involution of economic growth. As population grew, farmers steadily increased their output of grain, but only at the cost of constantly diminishing the rate of return for each hour of their labor. To use an analogy, they had to run faster just to stay where they were. The dead end of involution—growth of production without development of greater productivity per person—which had held Chinese farmers back for centuries, still held them back in the post–World War II era.

Similarly, the grand plan of equalizing the amount of money people in the city and the countryside earned had made little progress. One major reason was that different areas had different resources and different capacities for improvement. Farmers in a poor, rocky, mountainous region with little irrigation were condemned to poverty unless given a handout from outside. Rice farmers in the well-irrigated Lower Yangzi region would continue to have a higher standard of living. Another factor perpetuating inequality was the prohibition of rural migration to the cities. As a result, the city workforce became more fully employed and better off. That betterment spread to the countryside indirectly, but not to a great enough distance from the cities.

Post-Mao Agricultural Reforms

In approaching agricultural reform after Mao, planners recognized that rural management had been faulty, particularly in motivating the farmers. In the late 1970s, reform was tried first in the central Chinese province of Sichuan, as well as in Anhui, also in central China; nationwide there would be many variations in form and timing.

One important move was to encourage farmers to engage in sideline production, such as weaving or handicrafts, in addition to their primary task of grain cultivation. Farmers could sell the products of their sideline labor on free markets locally, which would raise their income. The major change, however, was the "production responsibility system." This meant that rather than dictating from above what farmers should produce and how they should work, the government brought the decision making back to the level of the production teams of, say, 25 to 40 families. Now the whole community could join in planning to maximize production (and to boost incomes).

The additional step of allotting individual farm families a specific parcel of land to cultivate further decentralized decision making, and it provided an incentive for farmers to work harder and more intelligently. Under this arrangement—called the *baogan*, or "full

The agricultural reforms of the late 1970s permitted families to sell their surplus grain or produce in order to earn extra money.

responsibility of the household," system—families were obliged to deliver a specified amount of crops to the production team (from which the state would continue to get its portion), and they had to contribute some of their labor to collective projects (such as the maintenance of irrigation systems). But whatever grain they produced in excess of the specified amount was theirs to consume or sell as they saw fit. Before, all crops harvested were pooled in a local pot, with individuals receiving equal rations regardless of the work they had done. Now, extra effort meant the chance to benefit personally.

This change of system had dramatic effects. Agricultural production and rural incomes shot up—a triumph for the Party's reforms. In the 1980s, rural production grew about two and a half times, far ahead of the population increase. This was due to the new motives of personal profit; new means in sideline production of poultry, fish, vegetables, fruit for the market, and the like; and new opportunities for work in local service industries.

The Limits of Reform

So what has the revolution ultimately achieved for the farm family? In the Maoist era, the door was opened to elementary education, public health, and improved technology. Furthermore, the doctrine of egalitarianism gave peasants a new view of themselves and their potentialities. On the other hand, the workload hardly diminished, and in some respects the landlord had simply been supplanted by the state in a new kind of feudal arrangement. Under Deng Xiaoping, millions of peasants became entrepreneurs. But in the big state-run industrial plants, Chinese Communist Party personnel opposed these small entrepreneurs and used the power of Party funding to reduce the number of entrepreneurial households in favor of cooperative enterprises. They were devoted to maintaining the big state-run plants as expressions of "socialism"—which, not coincidentally, gave them local power. Thus, while the years since 1949 have brought tremendous changes and upheavals to rural life in China, it might be argued that one thing has remained constant: the peasant has continued to lose out.

Sadly, that trend is likely to persist as industrialization spreads its reach further into rural areas of the country. As China becomes more integrated into the global economy, and more reliant on manufacturing and trade for its revenues, farmers in rural areas continue to be left behind. When China entered the World Trade Organization at the end of 2001, it promised to give foreign agricultural exporters the right to sell and distribute goods directly to consumers in China. The government would also lift taxes on rice imports while phasing out financial support for local rice and cotton farmers. How will the farmers of China survive in this new era? If recent unrest among farmers in the western Chinese province of Jiangxi is any indication of how other rural people feel, then the Chinese Communist Party might have to reexamine how it can help the group from which it has historically drawn its most loyal supporters—the peasants—without losing its ties to the global trading arena.

Government and office buildings in Singapore, one of the so-called Four Asian Tigers (along with Taiwan, Hong Kong, and South Korea). The economic success of these capitalist neighbors helped convince Chinese reformers to steer their country toward a more market-based economy.

4 Economic Reform in China

By the time Mao died in 1976, the majority of the Chinese population—especially those in the villages—had become disillusioned with socialist governance. If the failure of the Great Leap Forward and the violent upheavals created by the Cultural Revolution were what Mao meant by socialism, the Chinese people were tired of it. Consider the anomalies coming out of Mao's great socialist experiment and the reasons would be apparent: class status, ascribed during the 1950s, had been inherited by the succeeding generation and now amounted almost to a caste system. Offspring of the 6 percent who had been classified in the Cultural Revolution as of the "four bad types" (landlord, rich peasant, counterrevolutionary, and bad element) lived under a permanent cloud. Meanwhile, mobility from countryside to city had continued to be cut off. Ironically, under Mao—the son of peasants and the embracer of the peasant masses—rural life was disesteemed as inferior, uncivilized, and to be avoided. The collectivized rural economy had failed to produce more. Even the great achievements of the revolution in spreading primary school literacy, road transport, and communication by press and radio had partly backfired by the end of the Mao era, revealing how much further China still had to go. Mao and his Communist Party may have been able to live up to their mission of ending foreign imperialism, but with that, they also ended foreign stimuli.

By the late 1970s China was ripe for economic reform. The unpopularity of the Cultural Revolution had left tremendous mistrust of the Communist Party and its ability to get the country back

Deng Xiaoping, the principal architect of Chinese economic reform, shakes hands with U.S. president Jimmy Carter after signing a formal diplomatic agreement, January 31, 1979. Deng understood that China's economy would develop only by attracting foreign technology and capital.

onto its feet. Deng Xiaoping, who succeeded to leadership of the Party in 1978, had to delicately distance the Party from the old regime and make changes to win back the support of the people.

Beyond the disaster of the Cultural Revolution, there were other reasons the country was ready for reform in the late 1970s. After years of experience in economic planning, government officials understood the shortcomings of the current system and grasped the need for change. Successful economic development in other parts of Asia—including Taiwan, Hong Kong, Singapore, and South Korea (known in the 1980s as "the Four Asian Tigers")—demonstrated to Chinese government officials and the Chinese people that a market economy worked better than a planned socialist structure based on communal sharing and tight controls over production. This lesson was reinforced by the different rates of economic development between Communist North Korea and capitalist South Korea, and between countries in Soviet-dominated Eastern Europe and countries in Western Europe.

From 1978 onward, the Chinese Communist Party was determined to correct its past economic mistakes and bring China back into the world economy. The transition from a socialist economic structure to a more market-oriented one would not be an easy task. The journey toward China's eventual admittance into the World Trade Organization, the chief international regulatory body on trade, would be bumpy and uneven.

A New Era of Looking Outward

Renewal of the Chinese Communist Party's claim to legitimacy required group leadership in the Party's Central Committee. After 1978 Deng, though dubbed "paramount leader," ostentatiously remained only a vice premier in formal status. Class struggle gave way to economic reform and development. The Maoist slogans "Politics in command" and "Red over expert" were supplanted by the ancient

The Patriarch of Economic Reform

Deng Xiaoping told a group of journalists in 1985 that in order to bring peasants into the political economy, it would first be necessary to give them the power to make money. This would be the mantra of Deng's reign over China from the late 1970s through the mid-1990s.

Born in 1902, Deng would follow a different path to communism than his predecessor, Mao Zedong. Deng was among the intellectuals who, while studying abroad in the 1920s, discovered Soviet Marxism and adopted the belief that it was the right system for China's future.

Now commonly known as the patriarch of China's economic reforms and the engineer for China's reemergence in the global economic arena, Deng had a checkered history with the Chinese Communist Party. A confidant of Mao's in the early 1950s, Deng was purged and condemned as a "capitalist roader" during the 1960s, at the beginning of the Cultural Revolution. It was only after Mao's death in 1976 that Deng returned to take the reins of governance in China.

statecraft dictum "Seek truth from facts." Ideology was downplayed.

The new day was heralded in foreign relations when the People's Republic turned outward again, welcoming foreign contact. Normalization of U.S.-China relations, begun in 1972 with U.S. president Richard Nixon's landmark visit to Beijing, was completed in January 1979. Deng's policy of "opening" acknowledged that the Chinese economy could progress only with a greater infusion of technology and capital from abroad. Unfortunately, industrial development was accompanied by major pollution problems. Laws to control these side effects existed, but, as in most countries, they were inadequately enforced.

By focusing on empowering the Chinese people—not with moral convictions as Mao did, but with economic means—the Party under Deng would lift more than 200 million people out of extreme poverty. Deng was also the first Chinese leader to tour the United States after World War II.

But his accomplishments were also marred by political ruthlessness. Scholars generally agree that it was Deng who ordered tanks into Tiananmen Square in June 1989, to break up pro-democracy demonstrations by Chinese students. The number of Chinese civilians killed in the crackdown will probably never be known for certain, but estimates range from a few hundred to several thousand.

After the Tiananmen incident, Deng pushed forward the most aggressive of his economic reforms, starting the process by which foreign companies could buy shares of ownership in Chinese companies, and forcing state-owned corporations to take more responsibility for their own business decisions. Deng's legacy is a mixed record, but even after his death in 1997 of Parkinson's disease, he would still be regarded as the leader who brought China into the global economic arena.

The ushering in of a new post-Mao era also meant a revival of the Four Modernizations (agriculture, industry, science and technology, and defense) initiated first in the 1960s but put on the back burner at the cusp of the Cultural Revolution. None of these modernizations promised any political reform. This was, as many scholars have argued, a deliberate gesture by Deng and the Party leadership not to reject the entire Maoist era, which would undermine the basic building blocks of China's post-1949 political and economic structure. Reform was one thing. Staging a new revolution was not a course upon which the Party was ready to embark. To preempt the subject of political reform and put it off limits in the usual Chinese bargaining style, Deng, in March 1979, issued the so-called Four Cardinal Principles that China must follow: the socialist path; the "people's democratic dictatorship"; the leadership of the Communist Party; and Marxism-Leninism–Mao Zedong Thought. Depending on one's point of view, the Four Cardinal Principles could be seen either as a way for the Chinese Communist Party dictatorship, like any dynasty, to maintain its monopoly on power, or as a way to give China the political stability it needed to undertake major changes.

Reformulating the Economy

The Deng regime's first need was to reestablish the Party's right to rule by acknowledging its errors. It tried to reconsider and correct wrong judgments inflicted on several categories of people, including millions of landlords and rich peasants in the early 1950s; the 500,000 or more persons purged for their supposed anti-proletariat sentiments in 1957–1958; several million in the countryside named "antisocialist elements" in the early 1960s; and at least 3 million Party members wrongly judged and 300,000 others wrongly convicted of crimes during the Cultural Revolution. Together with their families, they totaled perhaps 100 million people. Deng understood that the country's economic engine could not move forward unless the Party dealt with its tumultuous political past.

Among China's most pressing needs in the post-Mao era was to raise the rate of economic growth. During the period of the First Five-Year Plan (1953–1957), growth had been fairly rapid, reaching almost 9 percent annually by some measures. But since then, the Great Leap Forward, the failure to initiate the Four Modernizations in the late 1960s, and the Cultural Revolution all threw economic growth off course, slowing it to less than 5 percent a year. This not only widened the economic distance between China and its Asian neighbors, such as Hong Kong, Taiwan, and Singapore, but also highlighted for the country the disparity between the living standards and technological know-how of China versus other Chinese societies.

Under the old economic system, China's ability to attract foreign investment and know-how was severely limited. In the 1950s all of China's imported technology came from the Soviet Union and the Eastern European countries because, in the midst of the Cold War, the Western nations had imposed an economic boycott on China. During the 1960s and early 1970s, China's capacity to import foreign technology was further constrained by its inability to increase its manufactured exports to earn foreign exchange, for under the old economic system, enterprises were neither interested in, nor really capable of, producing competitive exports for overseas markets.

The reforms under Deng, and later under his successor Jiang

Workers in a busy factory in Taiwan produce color television sets during the 1980s. As the economy of the country Chinese leaders consider a "renegade province" boomed, the People's Republic struggled to overcome the massive disruptions caused by the Cultural Revolution.

Zemin, can largely be divided into three stages. In the earliest stage, from 1979 to 1984, only partial reforms were carried out. Although some aspects of a market-oriented economy were introduced during this period, the Chinese Communist Party still held a tight grip over its "planned economy" model. Reforms during this period focused on institutional changes in the agricultural sector, which were directed primarily at improving peasant incentives by abolishing the commune system and empowering peasants to win property rights. Reforms in the urban sector were very modest and were largely confined to the streamlining of state-owned enterprises.

The country moved into a second wave of reforms in the mid-1980s, with the focus now shifting to the urban area. The Party's official goals now were to change the way resources were allocated, shifting some of the control from the central government to the free market. For example, the Party reduced its involvement in urban planning and gave private enterprises more autonomy and accountability. The government began to relinquish its control over how prices should be set for goods sold and bought in the market.

The comprehensive reforms in the second stage were briefly interrupted by the Tiananmen Square tragedy in mid-1989. The tragedy highlighted an issue with which the Chinese Communist Party had been grappling since embarking on reforms in the late 1970s—the great struggle between socialism on the one hand and the forces that Marxism denigrated as bourgeois and spiritual pollution on the other. The question arose as to what was left of Chinese communism when so much of Mao's ideas about the proletariat revolution had been destroyed in the political turmoil of the 1960s and were further undermined during the post-Mao reforms.

What Chinese Communist Party leaders also realized after the Tiananmen incident was that the reforms in which they had invested such high hopes since the late 1970s hadn't actually delivered the anticipated results. Runaway inflation, huge debts among state-

A massive crowd of pro-democracy protesters occupies Beijing's Tiananmen Square, May 1989. In early June, the Chinese government carried out a violent crackdown on the protesters, resulting in significant loss of life. The Tiananmen massacre, as the incident came to be called in the West, temporarily derailed Deng Xiaoping's economic reform efforts.

owned enterprises, poor infrastructure, and a backward banking system were just a few of the reasons for this. The attitude within the Communist Party had not shifted entirely with the urgency of economic reform. State-owned enterprises still struggled under the weight of bureaucracy and were plagued by the inefficient use of workers and resources. Some of Deng's rivals in the Party leadership were unwilling to relinquish too much control over businesses. They particularly rejected the idea of handing the reins of state-owned businesses over to entrepreneurs (who might be more nimble and knowledgeable at helping the mammoth state-run corporations compete with smaller enterprises on price, quality of products, and innovation). That steadfast grip on the economy made it inevitable that China's first reforms in the post-Mao era would be piecemeal and inconsistent. And it was not surprising, on the cusp of the

Tiananmen Square tragedy, that China was still mired in a socialist planned economy.

The Legacy of Deng's Reforms

In the end, however, China's reformists won out. At a media event in 1992, Deng swapped his customary Red Flag limousine (an exclusive perk of top Party leaders) for a golf cart at an amusement park in Shenzhen, at the time one of China's more economically vibrant cities. To scholars as well as members of the Communist Party, the signal was clear: Deng was ready to pull the country back into a reform mode three years after the Tiananmen massacre.

Drawing on successes in economic reform in other countries, from Western Europe to Southeast Asia, Deng's dictate in the new wave of reforms centered on a shift in ownership away from the state and into the hands of consumers, workers, entrepreneurs, and the people of China as a whole. In addition, he pushed through the restructuring of China's Central Bank, putting it in line with the monetary systems in the United States and Germany. He also created a social security system that would largely be financed by employees, modeled after a similar retirement scheme in the neighboring country of Singapore.

Under the new reforms, Deng accepted a course even he had been unwilling to embark on before: the transformation of state corporations. He urged these companies to form joint ventures with foreign investors so that they could be enlivened by foreign management skills and knowledge. Deng also mandated that wages be linked to actual work. Corporations in turn would pare down their workforces, meaning that thousands of workers would lose their jobs. In his policy speeches in the early 1990s, Deng painted a picture of reform that would actually allow the socialist economy and market economy to exist side by side. In 1992, Deng was still not ready to relinquish all control over state-owned enterprises, but he started to suggest the possibility of allowing private shareholders to buy a portion of ownership in the state companies.

Jiang Zemin, Deng's chosen successor, would continue the reform efforts by pushing even more aggressively for the privatization of state-owned enterprises. When Jiang took over the Chinese Communist Party, the majority of China's 118,000 state-owned industrial enterprises were losing money. State-sector debt was a huge burden on the banking system and a continuing drain on the Party's finances. Jiang advocated a greater role for market-oriented ideas such as privatization, competition, and technological innovation, in a way that would frequently expose the Chinese Communist Party's perennial dilemma: how to retain its socialist core while still promoting economic advancement.

In 2003, before Jiang handed over the reins to new leadership, he made one last push to solidify a market economy's place in the Chinese Communist Party. At its 16th Party Congress, held in 2002, the Chinese Communist Party admitted three businessmen into its membership, marking the first time it had ever allowed capitalists to participate in the political process. The election of entrepreneurs, in particular, was significant—a clear show of the Chinese government's priorities in business and economic liberalization. Along with the appointment of reform-minded new leaders, this development seemed to confirm that Deng's reformist vision was finally coming to realization.

饮食市场
创建文明

Colorful neon signs advertise businesses along a street in Shenzhen, Guangdong Province. In 1980 the government of China designated Shenzhen a special economic zone, in which foreign companies could establish factories to take advantage of China's inexpensive and skilled labor.

5

Industrialization: Leaps Forward and Back

China's industrialization policy developed on an aptly phrased socialist principle: "walking on two legs." Self-reliance was the basic idea behind the policy, introduced in the 1950s; the goal was to make what China needed to provide for the country.

With the Chinese Communists' military victory in 1949 over the rival Nationalists, people who had fled to rural areas to escape the chaotic fighting in the cities began to migrate back to urban areas. China's urban population grew rapidly, outpacing the rate of job creation, and city governments found themselves overburdened with unemployment, rising crime, and overcrowding. Party leaders realized that both rural

A worker operates machinery in a Chinese factory, circa 1955. During the 1950s and 1960s, China modeled its industrial policy on that of the Soviet Union, with centralized government control over factories and production.

and urban industries would need to be reformed to keep workers and potential new arrivals to the cities under control.

It was natural that the Chinese government would turn to the Soviet model for industrialization. After all, the two countries shared a common political system based on communism. The Russian approach to industrialization focused first on heavy industry, at the expense of agriculture. The central or local government would decide how much human and material resources should be invested and how much should be produced. Then the policy would be conveyed as a dictate to the individual enterprises that ran the factories in the form of detailed obligatory targets and rules, such as how much they had to produce and what percentage of their products the factories had to turn over to the central government. Individual corporations had virtually no power to make changes or develop their own business strategies.

The upside of centralized planning was that it enabled China to mobilize the large-scale resources from all over the country that would be necessary for rapid industrial growth, and leaders could marshal these resources whenever and however they chose. During the first years of Chinese centralized economic planning, production increased up to 10 percent; these rates outstripped the achievements of China's neighboring Asian countries, such as Japan and India.

But there is, of course, a downside to this protective system of centralized planning: a toll on efficiency. What this means, in simple terms, is that even when production levels are met, they are met for the wrong reasons. In China, factories met higher production targets set forth by the government not by improving the way they used resources and workers, but by simply recruiting more workers (which China's large population growth made possible). Since more workers meant a larger payroll, more money had to be funneled into the production process. And since the government owned the majority of corporations, it ultimately paid out the additional money. Often more money was spent making products than could be earned from the sale of those products—which created growing debts among the state corporations.

This situation eventually prompted the government, in the late 1970s, to decentralize decision making in China's state-owned companies. This effectively marked China's complete abandonment of the Soviet model of industrialization (which China had, in any case, modified over the previous decades). In addition to its inherent inefficiency, the Soviet model, not surprisingly, failed to work for China because of its overemphasis on heavy industry at the expense of agriculture, which presented political problems. China's communism, unlike the Soviet version, was built on the backs of the rural peasantry, and the Chinese Communist Party did not want to risk alienating its political base by favoring industry entirely over the agricultural sector.

Industrialization Under Mao

Industrialization had actually begun in China well before Mao and the Communists took control in 1949. During the 1920s and 1930s, the ruling Nationalist Party wove capitalist ideology into the way state-owned corporations were managed, and while Mao was determined to follow the model of collectivization—the sharing of benefits and burdens—that had been established in agriculture, initially he had to leave in place elements of capitalism. The fact was that Chinese Communist Party leaders across the land knew much more about agriculture than about industry. Most came from a peasant background. Their patriotism and personal ambition would lead them to set high goals for their industrial projects and to inflate the results without putting down a solid policy for sound and gradual development.

During the early years of Mao's industrialization scheme, China depended heavily on Soviet aid, both financially and in the form of technical expertise. That dependence on Soviet assistance came at a high price. Almost all Soviet financial contributions were in the form of loans, which had to be repaid, meaning added financial burden for the Chinese government. To be sure, Soviet technology was more advanced than Chinese technology, and on the whole the relationship with the Soviet Union proved of crucial value to China, even though rural industry (an area in which the Soviet government itself had little interest) was shortchanged. Ultimately, Chinese leaders would realize that they had to tailor their own industrialization program. It would be impossible to neglect the rural area because that comprised a vast majority of the economy, and furthermore the Party's political support lay with the farmers.

The overdependence on the Soviet Union led Chinese Communist Party planners to tweak their vision for the Second Five-Year Plan in 1956. They agreed that improving heavy industry

Chinese assembly-line workers manufacture consumer appliances for export in a factory in Shenzhen. China has become one of the world's leading manufacturing centers.

was important for the country's advancement and should receive more investment. But the planners also returned to the roots of Chinese communism—the rural masses. They believed that investment needed to be made in the countryside, for progress there could be essential to long-term progress in the cities. The planners also felt that large-scale plants would be less effective than smaller ones in the interior. Small local plants, though less advanced in technology, could use labor and materials on the spot, reduce transportation costs, and begin the industrialization of the countryside. Meanwhile, the planners wanted to be less dependent on Soviet aid. A final incentive arose from the fact that collectivization of agriculture had not noticeably increased production of grain and other farm products. It seemed that the growth of the enormous state bureaucracy had begun to impede economic growth. There was strong sentiment within the Party in favor of less centralization. However, the Second Five-Year Plan discussed in 1956 was never worked out to the point of publication. It was superseded in the spring of 1958 by the Great Leap Forward.

Post-Mao Industrialization

Deng's most spectacular reversal of economic policy in terms of industrialization was his "opening" to foreign trade, technology, and investment. In the perspective of China's foreign relations since as far back as the 1800s, this was a swing of the pendulum. Before the unequal treaties of the 1840s and 1850s with Western imperial powers, China's Qing dynasty had regarded foreign trade and contact as inconsequential. For the Chinese Communist Party, a doctrine of self-reliance had at first been a part of the wartime economy.

Even in the late 1970s, China's investment policy continued to be a rather simpleminded copying of the Soviet model. The basic assumptions were, first, that the ratio of the amount of money put in to the amount of goods produced was fixed (meaning that an increase in investment from one year to the next would inevitably result in a predictable increase in production); and second, that foreign trade, and production of consumer goods for export to secure foreign capital, were unimportant (following the Chinese Communist mantra of anti-imperialism).

As time went on, the system started showing its flaws. The ratio of capital to output gradually rose—that is, it took more money to produce only a slight increase in the quantity of goods. When the national income growth rate fell and the investment rate continued to rise, the amount left for consumption could hardly grow. Production was also held back by the diversion of funds to defense for the Korean War (1950–1953) and the Cold War, and by a decline in worker incentives. Moreover, China's industrial equipment was old and inefficient, some 60 percent of it in need of replacement. Problems of management included overzealous central planning and an overemphasis on the sheer quantity of goods produced rather than the quality. Often there was too much supply and not enough market demand from consumers willing to buy those products. The net result was money lost.

By the 1970s, the Chinese economy was plagued by the classic problems of uneven industrial production and lack of concern for consumer demand characteristic of a centralized, command economy. The Five-Year Plan proposed in 1978 was unrealistically theoretical and impractical, and it reflected a desperate lack of understanding of basic economics. For example, the Daqing oil field in the northeast had become a major producing center, so the government plan called for 10 more such oil fields to be developed—regardless of whether or not there was any more oil that could be extracted. Not until 1979 did the planning strategy make a basic shift to emphasize agriculture and consumer goods for sale abroad. Part of that was driven by Deng Xiaoping's general opening up of the Chinese economy after he took control of the Party.

Deng's industrial reforms, strictly speaking, could not be termed a revival of capitalism, since the Party and the state still called the tune and remained devoted to the idea of collectivism (that is, socialism). Under the responsibility system in industry, however, the Party slowly released some of its power to managers at state corporations. State enterprises, instead of returning all their profits (and losses) to the government, now managed their own accounting, and though they paid a high income tax on their profits, they retained the rest for reinvestment in machinery or the building up of amenities and services for employees. This greater autonomy of enterprises and the more open market naturally gave workers increased incentives to be more productive.

Changing Management Practices

One flaw in the old system had been the tendency of Party members to exaggerate their production results in order to get more funding from the government. Beginning in the 1980s, the government tried to control this inefficiency by changing the way it funded industrial projects. Instead of giving one-time grants, the new policy was to give the money in smaller installments in the form of loans, and to charge interest on the money. Repayment of the loans became an incentive for project managers to be cognizant of their costs and to focus more on concrete ways to raise production.

Although the Party decentralized the task of business management, it still tightly controlled the pricing of goods, thus preventing the free play of market forces. This halfway decentralization created intense competition among local governments to keep costs down in order to increase their profit margins, leading to a great deal of illegal business activity that did nothing to improve the efficient use of resources or labor productivity.

China's Industrialization Today

Shanghai, China's commercial capital, is today surrounded by special economic zones that the government began to create in the mid-1980s in order to encourage foreign investment. The first special economic zone, located at Shenzhen, borders Hong Kong in southern China. Within the zone, foreign investors could set up factories to take advantage of inexpensive and skilled labor; wages there were determined largely by competition with other investors, in contrast to other parts of China, where wage rates were set by the Chinese government. Investors in the Shenzhen economic zone also received special tax breaks. In less than a decade, Shenzhen developed from

A shopper looks over Haier air conditioners at a store in Guangzhou. A manufacturer of appliances and electronics, Haier has set up factories and offices in more than 100 countries and is working to establish its brand internationally.

a piece of farmland into a modern city. Because of the difference in economic opportunities, citizens of China could enter Shenzhen only with special permission. Soon other economic zones and special areas were created for the convenience of foreign investors. By 2003 companies with foreign investors accounted for more than 50 percent of China's exports. What a difference from the collectivization and anti-imperialist policies of Mao's China!

All these changes began in the 1990s, under Deng's later reforms, when the Chinese Communist Party finally gave state-owned companies the right to control their own purchases, production plants, hiring of workers, and finances. Entrepreneurs, meanwhile, were allowed to set up businesses on their own or in the form of collectives. The typical collective started as a shareholding enterprise divided among three or four families from a local village and operating under the auspices of the village or county government. Among the so-called collectives now are multibillion-dollar groups with global operations.

Greater freedom has proved more of a challenge to state-owned companies; many of these enterprises failed to seize the opportunities presented to them. Their role in the Chinese economy has shrunk accordingly. Their share of China's gross domestic product—the total annual output of the country, including government spending, consumer spending, and business investments, among other factors—decreased from 80 percent in 1978 to less than 30 percent in 2000. With the shift in the political and economic tide, Chinese state corporations have been less able to rely on the not-so-hidden hand of the government to sustain them through good times and bad. Even the most famous companies have fallen by the wayside as a result. China's department stores were among the first bankruptcies, even though they are still highly visible pillars of the society. In early 2002, Haier, a manufacturer of appliances and electronics and one of China's most respected state companies, came under attack for its expensive expansion in the United States at a time when it was losing its competitive edge at home.

China's industrialization over the last 50 years has been a roller-coaster ride of economic fallacies and political turmoil. Only in the past two decades or so has the industrial side of the economy started to bring about economic benefit for the country. Leaders in today's Chinese Communist Party recognize that their ability to retain power hinges on the economic success of the country. Some stresses and setbacks will be inevitable, but the important lesson the government seems to have taken away from its industrial experiment is that there is simply no shortcut to development. How the future plays out will depend on how the government juggles its political socialism with its economic capitalism. In the particular context of the country's membership in the World Trade Organization, the story of China's industrialization is not yet over. The reform of the auto industry, for example, is a tale still to be told.

BANK
OF
CHINA

Until the reforms initiated by Deng Xiaoping, the People's Bank of China was the country's only bank. Decentralization of the banking and finance sectors, begun in 1979, has accelerated recently because of China's WTO obligations.

6 Banking and Finance

"To get rich is glorious." Deng Xiaoping spoke these words as he charted a course of economic reform for China in the post-Mao era. Deng recognized that the Chinese Communist Party in the late 1970s had to face the reality that even socialism needs money.

Until Deng's economic reforms, China for the most part had a rigid, monolithic, Soviet-style banking system—not unlike other parts of the Chinese economy at the time. All flow of money within the country (not much was flowing out, with the exception of trade with the Soviet Union) was monitored under the auspices of the People's Bank of China. The bank acted not only as China's central bank (equivalent to the U.S. Federal Reserve Bank), but also handled almost all of the applications from corporations to borrow money for business projects. Not surprisingly, there were no private banks in China.

The People's Bank of China had three branches—specialized banks, in essence—that negotiated the business comings and goings in specific sectors of the economy: the Agricultural Bank, the People's Construction Bank, and the Bank of China. Although these organizations were banks in name, they were in reality just agents for the Party to distribute the budgets among the various industries. They also acted as mediators between corporations and the central bank. For example, the People's Construction Bank of China, founded in 1954, was in fact the cashier for the Capital Construction Finance Department of the Ministry of Finance; it was used to pass out grants approved by the government for various infrastructure projects around the country. The Bank of China, established in 1949, was in fact the international business department of the People's Bank of China. All the savings of state enterprises had to be held in accounts at the People's Bank. All business transactions between corporations had to be settled through the People's Bank according to the state mandate. Salaries for workers employed by the state corporations could be passed out only through a separate "wage fund"; moreover, the Party set a quota on the fund in terms of how much cash could be withdrawn at a time. The bank diligently supervised each withdrawal. In short, the Chinese banking system was a structured and rigid system constructed with one purpose: to manage and control the money flow within the Party.

The existence of a centralized banking system in China also meant that the People's Bank of China had little independence from the executive branch of the government. In fact, the Law on the People's Bank explicitly stipulated that the People's Bank was subject to the monitoring of the state council. From the point of view of Chinese leaders, the argument seemed sound at the time. If economic policy and planning was an important responsibility of the state, then why shouldn't the management of the flow of money be a part of that responsibility as well? Placing the central bank under the control of the Party enabled the government to better coordinate its monetary and economic policies. Political influence may be bad for economic planning sometimes, but it may also be necessary at other times, the Party leadership argued.

Decentralizing the Banking System

The centralized system remained in place until 1979, when the three specialized banks under the central bank broke off from its control (although they remained under the overall control of the government). The government began allowing foreign banks to operate in China in the early 1980s. Nanyang Commercial Bank, a Bank of China Hong Kong affiliate, became the first "foreign" bank to offer banking services, in Shenzhen. In 1984 the People's Bank of China became China's official central bank, focusing on currency control and monetary policy. Its remaining commercial lending operations were consolidated into a new bank: the Industrial and Commercial Bank of China, now China's largest bank.

In 1985, many small Chinese banks were created. By the 1990s, these smaller banks had begun to grow and accounted for more than 10 percent of the savings. This gave them a substantial presence, but they were still not a threat to the dominant position of the People's Bank of China. In 1994, Beijing passed the Commercial Banking Law, which made it a crime for local officials to pressure banks to make policy loans. The government created three policy banks to assume responsibility for directed lending and policy loans from the government, typically for state-owned corporations. In 1995, the government reached a further milestone in its attempt to loosen up the financial industry. The government told the three former arms of the People's Bank of China, plus the Industrial and Commercial Bank of China, that they were now expected to operate as proper commercial banks, responsible for their own profits and losses.

The U.S. banking giant Citibank is one of many banks attempting to make inroads into the Chinese market. Citibank has also helped the Bank of China improve its business management practices.

However, independent commercial practices among the state banks were slow to take hold even with the gradual introduction of competition. Since the founding of the central planning system, the state banks had been largely immune from market pressures. With periodic government bailouts for financial mistakes, the banks had never been held accountable for making bad decisions about lending money to certain business enterprises. Requiring that they suddenly begin operating like any commercially viable bank would represent a 180-degree change in policy and create a business environment with which the banks were simply not equipped, structurally or culturally, to deal.

For years, everything had been controlled at the higher state level, and the individual bank executives had no incentive or pressure to improve the quality of their decision-making processes or to learn from past mistakes. At the same time, Party officials routinely applied political pressure or offered bribes to bank executives for special favors, such as obtaining a loan or an extension on the repayment of a loan, regardless of the merits of the request. As a result, China's state banks were weighed down—and some still are—by bad loans made out of political pressure or personal greed. Frequently, loans made to individuals and corporations under these circumstances were never repaid.

Realizing the importance of a sound financial system for the country's economic future, the government has in recent years tried to restructure the banking sector more aggressively. One measure was the announcement that the banks would be privatized through stock market listings, meaning that shares of ownership of the banks could be sold on the stock market to private investors. This move was meant to make the bank executives more accountable in the way they formulate policy and make decisions about loans and savings. At the same time, in 2001, the government issued special bonds to raise money to help the big-four state banks deal with bad loans. In addition, the government has, over the years, been carefully designing an opening of the banking sector to private and foreign participation. Private investors may now set up banks in cities where there are no local banks and may acquire partial ownership (by buying shares) in some of the local banks.

These measures have sent a clear signal to executives of the big-four banks that they must reform their institutions to make them better equipped to function in a competitive environment. From province to province, the banks are starting to offer better services to their customers, such as financial advice, aided by almost unlimited consulting support from international banks. For instance, Citibank, one of the largest U.S. banks, has all but transferred its core business process management know-how to the Bank of China. The emergence of a new generation of banks in China—ones that lack the burdensome legacy of poor management and debt that the big four now carry—

provides an additional stimulus to all banks to modernize. Progress may be slow, but consultants working with the banks say that reforms are beginning to take shape.

Playing the Stock Market

Part of reforming the financial system of China and shifting it away from the socialist ideals of the Mao era involved opening up the markets to foreign investment. With this came the establishment of financial institutions such as stock exchanges, whereby private citizens can buy shares of ownership in certain companies. In 1990, both Shanghai and Shenzhen opened their stock exchanges with great fanfare. In 1992, the government established a formal regulatory body—the China Securities Regulatory Commission—indicating the priority it was giving to strengthening the financial sector. In 1993, Tsingtao Brewery became the first Chinese company to be traded on the Hong Kong Stock Exchange.

To maintain a certain degree of control over the financial sector even as the country shifts toward a more market-driven economy, the Chinese government imposed restrictions on which corporations could be listed on the stock exchanges. The regulatory body for the stock exchanges assigned quotas to the planning commissions of various provincial governments, permitting the commissions to decide which corporations were worthy of being listed on the stock exchanges. The planning commissions, not surprisingly, filled their quotas mainly with state-owned enterprises.

But China's ambitions to rise to the stature of a world economic power trumped many of the controlling mechanisms. As a condition for its acceptance into the World Trade Organization, China agreed to begin introducing measures, in July 1999, designed to loosen the Party's grip on the stock exchanges and to move the exchanges toward international standards. The quota system for companies wanting to list on the exchanges had to be abolished

A view of the interior of Beijing's stock exchange. During the late 1990s China introduced measures that brought the country's stock exchanges closer to compliance with international standards, and in 2001 foreigners were permitted to invest in China's stock markets for the first time.

and replaced with an expert-review panel. Now a one-year preparatory phase is required before a company may file an application to be listed on a stock exchange. Investment banks must submit these applications on behalf of candidates, and selected members from an 80-member expert committee review the qualifications of the candidates. Starting in 2001, the regulators began allowing foreigners access to the domestic stock markets in China.

Financial Sector Reform

The Asian financial crisis of 1997, which created economic mayhem all over the region, served as a wake-up call for the Chinese government to clean up its financial sector. The established and

China's WTO Commitments in the Financial Sector

Banking:

Foreign banks permitted to conduct local currency business with Chinese companies starting in 2004

Foreign banks permitted to offer services to Chinese individuals by 2006

Foreign banks given the same rights as Chinese banks within specific parts of the country by 2006

Securities (companies that manage stocks and funds):

Foreign companies to be permitted to have a small share of ownership in local Chinese securities firms

Insurance:

Foreign companies allowed to offer insurance for large-scale risks by 2006

Foreign insurers allowed to offer services in health and pensions by 2006

Foreign insurers to be permitted to own 50 percent of a Chinese company for life insurance

Sources: Information compiled from the WTO website and various government websites for the Chinese government.

successful economies of many of China's neighbors, including South Korea, Hong Kong, and, to a lesser extent, Taiwan, were rocked; the value of national currencies plummeted, stock markets collapsed, and a host of companies declared bankruptcy.

China's economy performed quite well during the Asian financial crisis, which is remarkable considering that China shared some of the economic vulnerabilities that afflicted its neighbors, including a weak financial system and poorly performing state corporations. Ironically, it would be the Party's tight control over the economy that helped China weather the crisis. Even so, Party leaders were motivated to accelerate reforms so that they might forestall future financial crises.

The financial reforms of the late 1990s were wide-ranging, from increasing the basic transparency of the system (so that corporations and foreign investors can understand the full picture of where their money is being used) to reducing government interference in investment and business decisions. There were mergers and closures of ailing credit cooperatives, remnants of China's more socialist past. New regulations were introduced to force corporations to be more responsible in their accounting practices, so that the information on costs and earnings would be accurate and up-to-date for potential investors, both domestic and foreign. The government also publicly acknowledged the extent to which the country's financial system was suffering from bad loans.

With China's entry into the World Trade Organization, these reforms are only going to continue—and they will occur under the watchful eye of the international community. Foreign banks will soon be able to set up full banks in China. Foreign insurance companies can currently operate only in Shanghai and Guangzhou, a city in southern China. But with its WTO ascension, China will begin to lift the geographical restrictions on foreign insurance companies. These companies will slowly be able to buy a share of ownership in already successful local companies.

Unlike agricultural reforms, which have systematically been implemented for more than three decades, China's financial changes are just beginning. But these reforms will be perhaps the most crucial component of China's transformation from a socialist economy into a capitalist, market-oriented system.

世界人民大

A young woman chats on her cell phone in Beijing. Information technology has been a key part of China's economic strategy, but a freer exchange of information with the outside world poses a potential threat to the Communist Party's political control.

7 Developing the Tech Sector

One of the main goals of the economic reform process started in 1978 by Deng Xiaoping was to raise China's domestic technological capabilities. Like their counterparts in other developing countries, Chinese leaders had been dissatisfied with, and unwilling to accept, their place in the international division of labor. They wanted to leave behind industries dependent on low labor costs and second- or third-generation technologies, gradually shifting the focus to high-technology industries, which offer the most lucrative opportunities. China was not content to remain a consumer of the newest technologies produced by more advanced economies. It wanted to be as close to the cutting edge of technological innovation as possible; it wanted to harness not only the economic but also the political, military, and social benefits that accompany technology-intensive development. Put in Deng's words, China expected to take its place in the world.

Students of Chinese history would find a little irony in the fact that China had to scramble to catch up with the rest of the world in the 1990s. For centuries imperial China thought of itself as the "Middle Kingdom," the center of the world, and regarded all cultures outside its borders as "barbarians" who had nothing worthwhile to offer. And over the course of its history China had made important technological advancements, including paper, printing, gunpowder, and the compass. In a sense, Mao's Great Leap Forward (1958–1962), during which the peasant masses were mobilized to melt metal pots into industrial materials, was an attempt to demonstrate to the world China's technological capabilities. But it failed dismally.

The Four Modernizations policy, announced in 1964, gave science and technology a prominent role. But the chaos wrought by Mao's Cultural Revolution, which began two years later, brought the ambitious plans for technological innovation to a grinding halt. Later, when Chinese leaders again attempted to focus on science and technology and create a culture of innovation, they found themselves confronting a huge challenge: a dearth of talent. The Cultural Revolution and other Mao-era political purges of intellectuals had squeezed China dry of qualified researchers and scientists equipped to help advance the country's technological capabilities. So first on the agenda for China's technological revolution was training.

Reviving a Technology Culture

Until the reforms of 1978, what technological development that did occur in China was based entirely on the Soviet model. Although China attained notable successes in the fields of computer, nuclear, and aviation technologies in the 1950s and early 1960s, the highly hierarchical and stratified structure of the science and technology establishment limited the scope and range of these

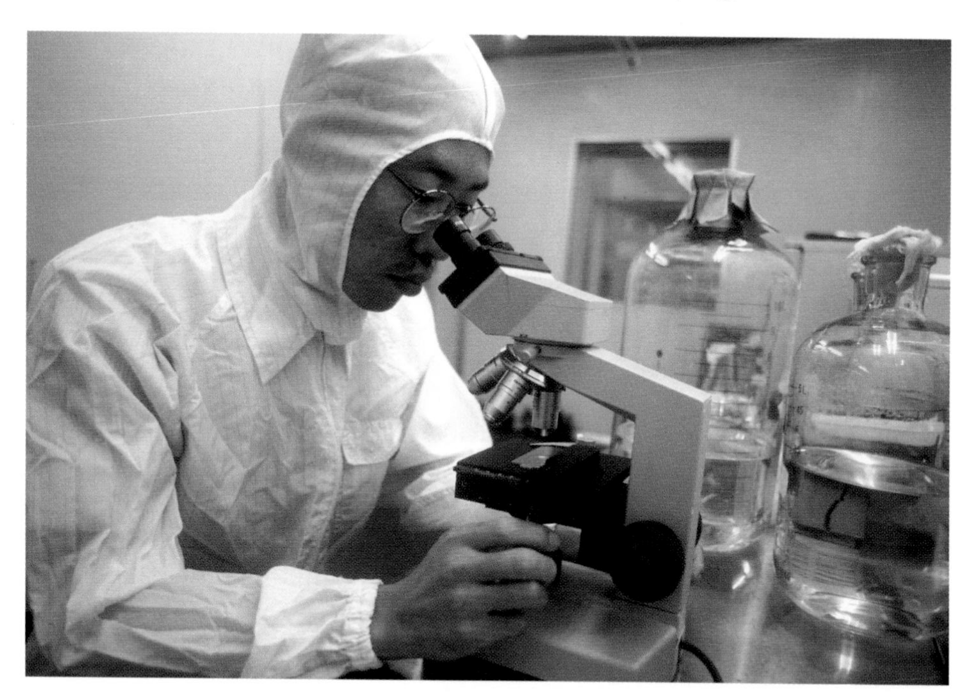

A technician peers into a microscope in a laboratory in the Shenzhen Science Park. After 1978 China focused more resources on the training of researchers in science and technology.

achievements. Research and development took place in diffuse locations, with no coordination between them. Industrial ministries possessed their own autonomous research laboratories, and even these institutions communicated infrequently with one another. Moreover, labs within state-owned corporations operated under an administrative structure that put excessive emphasis on indicators of quantitative output rather than technological advances.

The reforms of 1978 set out to address some of the ideological and institutional barriers to economic and technological development. For starters, the Party realized it needed a force of skilled researchers to achieve any kind of development in high-priority areas of technology such as energy sources, computers, laser and space technology, genetics, and physics. So it organized a crash training program for 800,000 scientific research workers and set up a network of new research centers integrated into a national system.

Over the following months, policies were drawn up for the establishment of 88 "key universities," with admission only by rigorous competitive examinations, as well as a number of lower-track technical colleges. Schools were instructed to identify gifted children early and give them advanced training. Scientists sent to the countryside during the Cultural Revolution were recalled and reassigned to professional jobs. The Chinese Academy of Sciences was reinvigorated, as was the Science and Technology Commission.

Even more urgent was the need for a practical linkage between research and production. In 1984 a survey of 3,500 scientific institutes throughout China showed that less than 10 percent of "scientific achievements" had been applied to production, meaning that the ideas the scientists came up with never got put into practice. The following year, the Party leadership called for the creation of "organic links" between research and production. On the pages of scientific journals and at conferences, more than 100 professional organizations discussed ways to combat the old tendency of research units to hoard their talent competitively and duplicate work already done by others.

Meanwhile, the Party's central leadership struggled to manage China's sprawling technology sector. It was unclear who within the government oversaw the development of the sector. In addition to the academies, nearly 5,000 research institutes fell under the monitoring of the government ministries and the provinces, and still others came under the authority of universities. Financing was aided, for the most part, by contracts between institutes and corporations, taking full advantage of the market to secure funding for technological innovation. This effectively brought the more outlying regions of China into the new technology promotion policy.

On the broader level of technological development, dramatic advances were achieved as the result of Deng Xiaoping's "open door policy," by which China brought in advanced foreign technology and management techniques in return for access to China's domestic market. The earliest investment projects were carefully chosen to raise the level of expertise in key areas such as oil production. Along with this opening, the central government also loosened the grip of business ownership in urban areas. Local governments, administrative departments, and a wide range of public institutions were given greater authority over how to spend their budgets, particularly in the technology sector. Freed from having to meet production quotas handed down from above, corporations could now actively exploit market opportunities.

The Information Technology Boom

Like many industrializing countries, China eyed the emergence of the Internet in the 1990s as a prime opportunity to level the playing field in technological advancement. Information technology became the priority of China's tech strategy in the 1990s.

To succeed, however, the strategy would have to overcome a major hurdle: China's "brain drain." Many Chinese computer scientists and software engineers were working in foreign countries, often after having obtained advanced degrees in those countries. For instance, numerous Chinese were employed in California's Silicon Valley, whose small start-up companies appeared to be driving much of the Internet boom.

To lure young entrepreneurs home, local governments throughout China began setting up special centers that offered free rent and other benefits. Beijing, for example, announced the establishment of a Silicon Valley recruitment center in a bid to attract students to return to China after their studies. Different ministries began to provide broad support for domestic enterprises designated "high technology." This support took the form of access to low-interest credit lines, preference in procurement decisions, or other kinds of regulatory preference or relief. At the same time, the government began catering to the specific needs of smaller technology companies. The new policy established a fund to support innovation by small and medium-sized companies and gave preferences for domestic high-tech products. It also gave companies tax deductions for research; provided a tax exemption for foreign companies that transferred or developed new technologies with domestic firms; and offered tech companies priority listing on the Shanghai and Shenzhen stock exchanges.

These measures paid big dividends. During the 1990s the information technology (IT) sector registered the fastest growth rates among all of China's industrial sectors. By 2000 China's domestic IT market was worth $168 billion, nine times more than it had been worth at the beginning of the 1990s. By 2005 China's leaders expected to have invested $500 billion in the sector, raising the contribution of IT to gross domestic product to 5 percent.

But if the IT boom offered China large economic benefits, it also presented a thorny political problem for the Chinese government. The spread of the Internet made it extremely difficult to control the dissemination of ideas, information, and opinions—including criticism of the Chinese government's policies—which threatened the very comfortable autocratic state system that the Chinese Communist Party enjoyed.

Not that the Chinese government hasn't tried to control the flow of information. According to a Harvard University survey in late 2002, more than 19,000 of 250,000 websites tested were blocked in China. These websites included the search engine Google and the British Broadcasting Corporation (BBC) news site. While access to these sites was later restored, content is still filtered. Such censorship efforts illustrate the Chinese government's continuing dilemma: on the one hand, it wants China to be among the world's most technologically advanced nations; on the other hand, it wants to keep a tight political grip on the Chinese population.

Still, Yahoo! and Google have said they would be happy to

Legend Computers: Learning Lessons from Foreign Investors

When people in most parts of the world want to buy a personal computer, they usually think first of the well-known brands: Compaq, Dell Computer, and IBM, for example. Not so in China. There the PC of choice is called Legend. Never heard of it? Perhaps not for long, if Liu Chuanzhi has his way. Since 1984 Liu, the chairman of Legend Holdings, has built his company into China's (and Asia's) number-one manufacturer of PCs, with more than $3 billion in annual revenue. Legend expects to double that figure by 2006. Although still controlled by the state, Legend is listed on the Stock Exchange of Hong Kong, open to private investors who want to buy shares in the company and, to some degree, open to scrutiny for its business strategies. Started originally as a distributor of foreign computer brands, such as Hewlett-Packard and Toshiba, Legend has carved out a niche for itself.

What makes Legend, which just a few years back was losing money and on the brink of bankruptcy, now so competitive with foreign computer makers? Its local distribution network and its own computer stores definitely give it the upper hand. From its years as the distributor of HP printers, Toshiba notebook computers, and IBM minicomputers, Legend learned and absorbed valuable lessons about technology manufacturing processes and about how to organize sales centers and how to market products. Whereas Toshiba used to be a leader in the Chinese market in notebook computers, Legend's own brand now has surpassed its old distribution partner's sales figures, making the company a clear example of how China has benefited from foreign investment.

comply with regulations set by the Chinese government. For these companies—and for many other foreign investors—access to 1.2 billion consumers offers too great a potential reward to be deterred by a bit of restrictive government control. Among the businesses aggressively trying to capture a share of the Chinese technology market is the software giant Microsoft. On a business trip to Beijing in March 2003, Microsoft founder Bill Gates agreed to show Chinese officials the underlying source code for the company's Windows operating system, in an attempt to reassure the Chinese about the product's integrity. In the face of increasing competition, Microsoft has found itself struggling to carve out a solid place in a Chinese market full of choices.

But in the long run, competition is something Microsoft knows how to cope with. The bigger unknown for Microsoft (and for other technology companies in China, for that matter) is whether its rights will be protected. Even as technological development has

Microsoft's second research center outside the United States, shown in this photo, is located in Beijing. Anxious to tap into the world's largest consumer market, the U.S. software giant—like other tech companies—has been willing to make concessions to the Chinese government.

thrived under China's economic reforms, the government has fallen short in one key area: controlling software piracy, the illegal copying and sale of copyrighted software products.

Intellectual Property Rights

China's software piracy rate hovers at a staggering 92 percent, with about $2.4 billion in illegal products churned out annually. Protecting intellectual property is one of the most discussed topics in U.S.-China trade relations. The issue is complicated by the fact that China has long done without a structured system for protecting intellectual property that involves patents, trademarks, and copyrights. The very notion of owning an idea had been somewhat foreign to China under the Communist system of sharing everything.

Still, the Party leadership has made an effort to incorporate the concept of protecting intellectual property into the consciousness of the Chinese people. Ironically, even as China has gained a better understanding of the reasons to protect intellectual property, piracy has grown into a multibillion-dollar industry. By the early 1990s Chinese intellectual-property pirates had become enormously successful producing, selling, and often exporting pirated material, primarily from Western countries. Most companies operating in China—not just those producing software—have stories of piracy to tell. Chrysler, for example, had knock-off artists producing illegal copies of its Jeeps.

After the United States threatened China with trade sanctions in 1992, the Bush administration concluded an agreement with China aimed at ending the piracy of intellectual property. Under the terms of the agreement, China adopted a complete set of intellectual property laws covering patents, trademarks, and copyrights. On paper, these amendments put China's intellectual property laws on a par with those of leading Western countries. The new Chinese statutes exceeded the minimum standard set by the World Trade Organization, and Carla Hills, then the U.S. trade representative, triumphantly proclaimed that China had adopted world-class intellectual property laws.

Unfortunately, the world-class laws changed little in practice. They were simply not enforced consistently. Between 1992 and 1994, piracy of intellectual property went from being a hidden cottage industry to a full-scale export industry. In southern China, dozens of factories pirated intellectual property, primarily U.S. films, recordings, and computer programs, on compact discs. The CDs were then exported to markets as far away as Eastern Europe, Canada, and the western United States. Computer programs worth thousands of dollars could be purchased for as little as $10 on the streets of Beijing.

In 1993, the Clinton administration took up the challenge of combating Chinese intellectual property piracy. In February of 1994, a deal was struck with the Chinese government that focused on

A street vendor sells pirated DVD copies of popular movies in Beijing. Piracy of intellectual property is rampant in China, and the United States and other WTO members have complained that the Chinese government has not done enough to crack down on the unauthorized production and sale of software, music CDs, videos and DVDs, books, and other products.

enforcing Chinese laws. Unfortunately this agreement, like its predecessors, also failed to stem the tide of piracy.

China made some efforts (critics characterized them as piecemeal and shallow) to crack down on piracy, but the primary effect was to put street-level dealers out of business. The factories, however, continued to operate. In fact, within a year of the 1994 agreement, new factories had opened and production of pirated goods had actually risen. After the United States threatened to impose about $2 billion in trade sanctions on China, the two countries reached a third understanding on intellectual property in the summer of 1996.

China does seem serious about cleaning up piracy. In 2003 Beijing, with the help of $750 million from Microsoft, agreed to track down software pirates. In September of that year, Chinese authorities seized tens of thousands of illegal programs in nationwide raids. Local and provincial courts are seeing more companies use China's intellectual property laws to sue other companies for copyright infringement. Judges, having received more training and education on what constitutes intellectual property, are now passing down judgments that further tighten copyright protection.

But while a change in laws and official attitudes toward intellectual property has been an important first step to curtailing piracy, challenges remain. China needs to develop a broad strategy for enforcing the laws and stopping piracy at its roots—at the factories that produce the illegal products. According to lawyers who work on intellectual property litigation, the software pirates remain difficult to hold accountable, even when Chinese courts order them to pay damages. A large percentage of the judgments for copyright violation go unenforced, and the companies whose products were stolen never see a penny of compensation. Until the Chinese government can remedy this situation, the technological revolution in China will not be complete.

永安珠寶金
WING ON JEWELRY L
龍門大酒樓
雙喜大茶樓
謝瑞麟
健體樂園
華僑商業銀行
中南銀行
AEG

Hong Kong, a British colony for more than 155 years, became a powerhouse of free-market capitalism even as China languished economically under strict Communist control. Since its return to China in 1997, Hong Kong has assumed increased importance as an intermediary in trade between China and Taiwan.

8

The Golden Triangle of East Asian Trade

Just a mile of choppy water separates Kinmen, an outlying island belonging to Taiwan, from Mainland China. On a clear day, the skyline of the Chinese coastal city of Xiamen is visible from Kinmen. Despite this proximity, there is no direct air travel between China and Taiwan—a restriction attributable to the long-standing feud over whether Taiwan is an independent country or a renegade province that broke away illegally from China. In fact, because of the ongoing political tensions, there was no way at all to travel directly between Taiwan and China until 2001, when the respective governments agreed to allow boats to go between Kinmen and Xiamen, as well as between Matsu, another outlying Taiwanese island, and Fuzhou, on the southeastern coast of China.

In spite of their often bitter political relations, however, the two Chinese societies are undeniably connected to each other economically, from the most traditional fishing industry to the most advanced high-technology sector. And Hong Kong, the former British colony that returned to China's fold in 1997, has become the intermediary. Together with Hong Kong, Taiwan and China form a rather imposing golden triangle of trade in the Asia-Pacific region.

At first it might seem strange that two capitalist, market-driven economies like those of Taiwan and Hong Kong have become so inseparable from Mainland China's still somewhat controlled economy. But the explanation lies less with economics than with cultural ties. For Hong Kong's population, access to China has always been a given. A train ride of less than three hours puts Hong Kong residents in Guangzhou, which in the 1980s was a vibrant economic hub for trade in southern China. For the Taiwanese, cultural ties to China remain strong. Many Taiwanese were separated from relatives when they fled Mainland China after the Nationalist Party's military defeat at the hands of the Communists in 1949. Continuing political tensions made communication and travel between Taiwan and the People's Republic of China almost impossible for the bulk of the 1950s through the early 1980s. Today, trade links offer many Taiwanese businesspeople an opportunity to reestablish connections with the people and places they left behind in China more than half a century ago. And of course, cultural similarities facilitate business dealings between Chinese and Taiwanese entrepreneurs, who share not simply a language, but also common expectations and a common etiquette of doing business.

Interestingly, China's transition to a more market-driven economy after 1978 was largely inspired by the successes of Hong Kong and Taiwan in establishing themselves in the world economy. Reform-minded Chinese leaders turned to these two close cultural and geographic neighbors—in particular, Taiwan—for a model of how to make a successful economic transition. In fact, China's post-1978 economic reforms share greater commonalities with the economic reforms that Taiwan initiated two decades earlier than the political leaders themselves would like to admit. Most obvious is the way in which the governments reduced their interference in business and encouraged private initiative. In the early 1950s, the Taiwanese government, run by the Nationalist Party, decided first to privatize agriculture and open the rural markets for exporting goods to other parts of the world. Taiwan opened its doors to foreign investors and trade much sooner than did Mainland China, giving it a certain leg up in the 1970s and 1980s, when toy and garment manufacturers flocked to Taiwan (and Hong Kong) for its low-wage workforce.

As Taiwan and Hong Kong moved into higher-end manufacturing and the cost of labor there rose, manufacturers searched for a new and cheaper place to produce clothes and gadgets. With its

Chinese workers assemble a Honda Accord at a plant in Guangzhou. China manufactured nearly 4.5 million vehicles in 2003, topping France as the world's fourth-largest producer.

FAST FACTS

TAIWAN

Population: 22.7 million (July 2004 est.)

Government type: multi-party democracy

Capital: Taipei

Currency exchange rate: 33.91 new Taiwan dollars = US $1 (September 2004)

Main exports: computer equipment, textiles, basic metals, equipment, plastic and rubber products, vehicles

Sources: CIA World Factbook, 2004; BBC Country Profiles; Bloomberg.com.

economic reforms treading steadily during the early 1990s, China became the natural replacement in the region for Taiwan and Hong Kong. Gradually, China—like Taiwan and Hong Kong before it—moved into more sophisticated technology sectors, such as the assembling of laptops and the manufacturing of computer monitors and memory chips.

Technology Exchange Across the Golden Triangle

A decade ago, local farmers were baffled as to why the city of Shanghai had decided to extend its No. 2 subway line across the Huangpu River all the way to their township of Zhangjiang, which at the time was a marshy expanse of rice fields and fish-filled canals less than an hour outside the city center. Many electronics

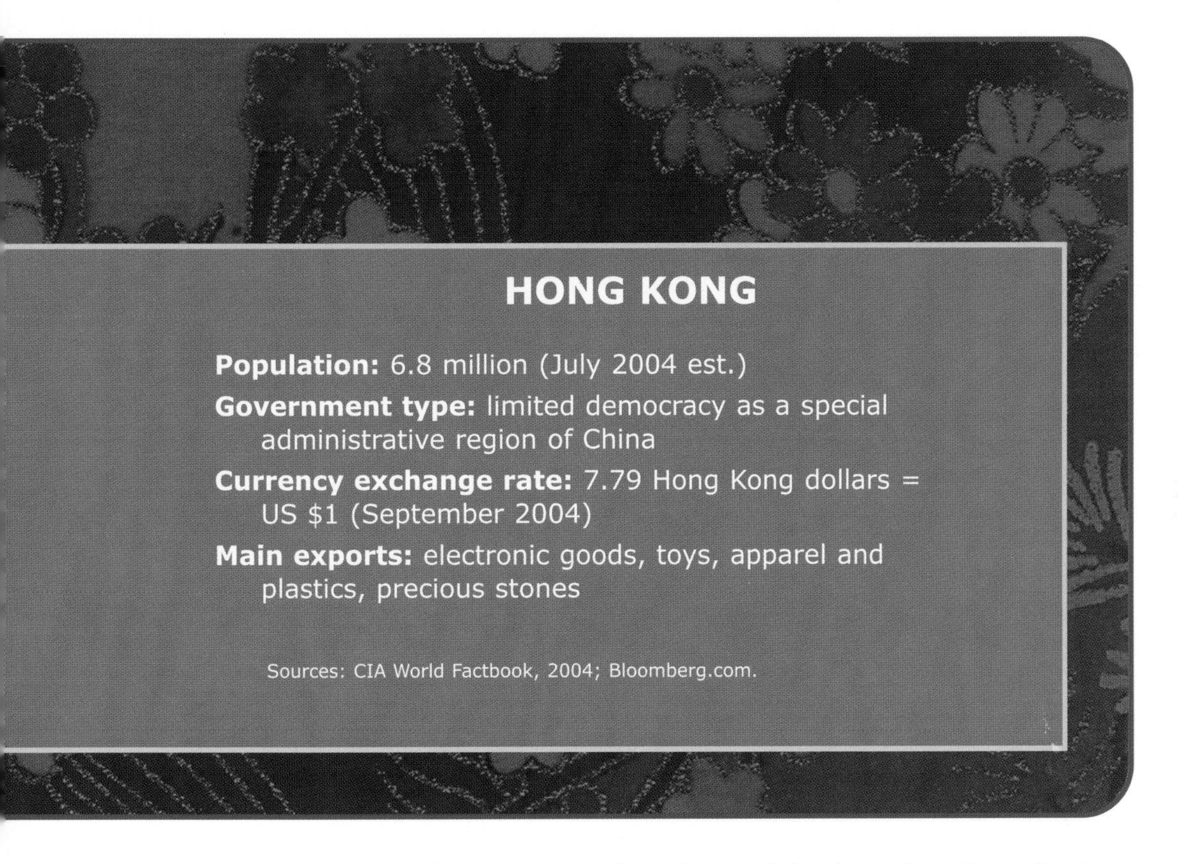

HONG KONG

Population: 6.8 million (July 2004 est.)

Government type: limited democracy as a special administrative region of China

Currency exchange rate: 7.79 Hong Kong dollars = US $1 (September 2004)

Main exports: electronic goods, toys, apparel and plastics, precious stones

Sources: CIA World Factbook, 2004; Bloomberg.com.

experts, meanwhile, regarded as laughable the official predictions that this site would become a high-tech park brimming with state-of-the-art semiconductor plants. The most likely investors, Taiwan's big chip manufacturers, were forbidden by their government from transferring such sophisticated facilities and technology to Mainland China.

Yet with stunning speed, this vision has become a reality. Taiwan's largest makers of computer chips invested billions of dollars in factories to manufacture delicate, highly sophisticated computer memory chips in the science park in Zhangjiang. As of early 2004, a total of 70 electronics companies had facilities in the zone, which also hosted research labs for other prominent foreign tech companies, such as Sun Microsystems, LG, and Sony. A 400-researcher lab by General Electric was on the way.

The science park at Zhangjiang is but a single focal point of one of the biggest economic mergers in history—as profound, perhaps, as the formation of the European Union. The concept of a Greater China has been developing since the 1980s, with the mass influx of manufacturers from Hong Kong, and then Taiwan, to the southern China coast soon after Beijing opened its doors. Hong Kong and Taiwan themselves started out as manufacturing hubs, but as their labor forces grew out of the low-wage jobs, it seemed logical to move those operations to China, where the country was just beginning to develop a niche in manufacturing.

With China's entry into the World Trade Organization in 2001, the industrial unification of the three economies has accelerated tremendously. Political barriers to investment in once-strategic industries such as semiconductors, oil, and banking are crumbling; infrastructure systems are fusing; and Hong Kong and Chinese officials are collaborating on regulatory affairs.

Developing a Greater China

Hong Kong maintained economic ties with Mainland China even when the former was a British colony, and it continues to play a crucial role in the development of the Greater China concept. Every morning, trains go between the two places, carrying fresh farm produce to the markets on both sides. In a bid to maintain the competitive edge of southern China's Pearl River Delta—which includes Hong Kong, Shenzhen, Guangzhou, Macao (also spelled Macau), and Zhuhai—over other parts of the country, business and government leaders in Hong Kong and Guangdong Province are discussing a $1.9 billion bridge that would connect Hong Kong to Zhuhai and Macao, rail and subway links, easier border crossings at Shenzhen, and ways to coordinate the services of the Delta's five airports.

Hong Kong's role as an international financial window for China is growing in importance. Major state enterprises such as the Bank of China are listed on the Hong Kong Stock Exchange, and the stocks of dozens of other companies are traded on Hong Kong's new second exchange, aimed at start-ups.

The impact of Greater China as an exporter can be felt across the globe. In just four years, the proportion of total world exports generated by Hong Kong, Taiwan, and Mainland China has risen from 6.9 percent to 9.6 percent, surpassing Japan, according to the World Bank. Economists predict that, by 2007, this proportion will reach 13.7 percent. Also by that year, as Mainland China and Taiwan open their markets to comply with WTO commitments, Greater China should pass $2 trillion in exports and imports (excluding trade between the three economies). That would make Greater China nearly twice the size of Japan as a trading power and two-thirds the size of the United States. In terms of purchasing

A view of containers packed with consumer goods ready for export at a busy shipyard in Hong Kong. China, Taiwan, and Hong Kong together ship nearly 10 percent of the world's exports—a figure that is expected to rise over the next few years.

power, the World Bank estimates that Greater China will overtake the European Union by the end of the first decade of the 21st century, by which time its combined gross domestic product will be nearly triple the size of Japan's GDP.

The real architects of this growing economic region are the entrepreneurs of Greater China and the officials in cities such as Shanghai, Shenzhen, and Hong Kong. They have spent two decades creating networks of influence and putting down roots, advantages that will be extremely difficult for foreigners to match. Equally important, these players are providing China with the managerial and financial expertise needed to compete in the world.

Why is this process speeding up? The biggest reason has been the economic reforms of Deng Xiaoping and his successors, Jiang Zemin and Hu Jintao. These reforms are now anchored even more firmly by China's entry into the World Trade Organization. Another reason is the ever-deeper integration of Hong Kong since the departure of the British in 1997. Securities regulators and monetary authorities from Hong Kong and Beijing now work closely with one another. Perhaps Hong Kong's most crucial role, though, is as Greater China's Wall Street. Chinese companies such as the Bank of China, which used to be shadowy presences in Hong Kong, now use it as a base to learn international management standards. InvestHK, a Hong Kong government body, has set up three teams dedicated to bringing Mainland China companies to Hong Kong. China's foreign trade ministry has also begun bringing delegations of private mainland entrepreneurs interested in opening Hong Kong offices. In the past, Hong Kong's main function was to send money to China for investment. Its role as an intermediary has broadened, however: it is now helping Chinese companies expand beyond the Greater China region.

Obstacles to Greater China Integration

The economies of China, Taiwan, and Hong Kong would all clearly benefit from full-fledged cooperation. But the political tensions between Taiwan and China continue to inhibit the free flow of trade among the three places. For example, Taiwan still bans the importation from China of thousands of products, from car engines to most farm goods. Trade is further hampered by the lack of direct shipping and air links, which turn a one-hour flight into a daylong ordeal transiting through Hong Kong. This greatly increases transportation costs. Economists estimate that removing all such barriers would add 3 percent to the economic growth of both Taiwan and China by 2011. It also would boost their combined exports by approximately $10 billion a year.

A plane lands at the airport in Hong Kong. Because of political tensions between Taiwan and China, there are no direct shipping routes between the two countries; instead, most goods must be shipped through Hong Kong. Experts believe that if the restrictions on direct trade between the two countries were removed, the economies of both would benefit.

China's Economy at a Glance

Gross domestic product (GDP*): $6.449 trillion (purchasing power parity)

GDP per capita: $5,000 (purchasing power parity)

Agriculture (14.5% of GDP): rice, wheat, potatoes, sorghum, peanuts, tea, millet, barley, cotton, oilseed; pork; fish (2002)

Industry and construction (51.7% of GDP): iron and steel, coal, machine building, armaments, textiles and apparel, petroleum, cement, chemical fertilizers, footwear, toys, food processing, automobiles, consumer electronics, telecommunications (2002)

Services (33.8% of GDP): government services, banking, tourism (2002)

Inflation: 1.2%

Unemployment: urban unemployment roughly 10%; substantial unemployment and underemployment in rural areas

Population below poverty line: 10% (2001 est.)

Foreign Trade:

Exports—$436.1 billion: machinery and equipment; textiles and clothing, footwear, toys and sporting goods; mineral fuels

Imports—$397.4 billion: machinery and equipment, mineral fuels, plastics, iron and steel, chemicals

Currency exchange rate: 8.28 yuans (also referred to as Ren minbi) = US $1 (September 2004)

*GDP = the total value of all goods and services produced in a year.

Unless otherwise indicated, figures represent 2003 estimates.

Sources: Adapted from CIA World Factbook, 2004; Bloomberg.com.

There are signs of increased collaboration, though. One such sign is the commingling of Taiwanese and Chinese banking systems. Beijing has recently allowed several Taiwan banks to open offices on the mainland, while two of China's banks have applied to do business in Taiwan. Even major government-owned companies are starting to cooperate in ways unimaginable until recently. Taiwan's China Petroleum Corporation, the largest oil company on the island, is jointly exploring for reserves with Beijing's China National Offshore Oil Corporation. And Taiwan's national airline, China Airlines, has won approval to buy a stake in the mainland's China Cargo in anticipation of new business with the establishment of direct flights.

As with any economic relationship, closer ties among China, Taiwan, and Hong Kong will always carry some potential hazards. For example, as Taiwanese and Hong Kong companies become more dependent on China for their manufacturing, components, engineering, and markets, they will become more vulnerable to a political or financial crisis there. Both remain distinct possibilities: China's banking system is in precarious shape, with an estimated $700 billion in bad loans as of 2004. Millions of angry workers with scant pensions are losing their jobs at state-owned industries, and labor protests are breaking out across the mainland.

There also is the possibility that political tensions could once again sour Taiwan-China relations. The Chinese government has consistently said it would reserve the possibility of military action against Taiwan to bring the island back into its political fold. As for Hong Kong, the primary worry is that the city's ineffective leadership will squander many of its advantages—a strong rule of law, good civil service, free media, and a tough anti-corruption stance—and blur the distinction with the mainland.

PERMANENT NORMAL TRADE
RELATIONS WITH CHINA

At an October 10, 2000, ceremony on the White House lawn, President Bill Clinton signs a bill establishing permanent normal trade relations with China. The legislation opened the way for U.S. companies to benefit from increased trade with China.

9

Post-WTO China: A Giant in the Making

For more than a century, China's promise as a trading and investment partner has lured foreign businesses in search of profits. From the owners of the great English cotton mills of the 19th century, who hoped that sales to China could keep their looms operating forever, to the executives of foreign telecommunications companies seeking to break into a potentially lucrative market in the mid-1990s, many have been disappointed. Part of the reason was poor planning by the Western firms. But a large part had to do with Chinese bureaucratic restrictions and limited market opportunities for foreign companies.

At the turn of the 21st century, however, China's economic future seemed brighter than ever. China had sailed through the Asian financial crisis of 1997 to 1998 relatively unscathed. Its trade was expanding at a record-setting pace, and the vast promise of its market for foreign firms was turning to reality in some sectors. Foreign manufacturers, led by Motorola and Nokia, had captured 95 percent of the market for cellular phones. Coca-Cola was the dominant supplier of carbonated beverages, with a market share 15 times that of its closest domestic competitor. McDonald's and Kentucky Fried Chicken, with almost 900 outlets in China between them, dominated China's rapidly growing fast-food market. Kodak had captured half the market for film and photographic paper. Volkswagen, through two separate joint ventures, controlled more than half the domestic automobile industry. And, as unlikely as it might once have seemed, Procter & Gamble, a company that makes toothpaste and toiletry products, claimed more than half of the world's biggest shampoo market.

How China Got into the WTO

In many respects, China's entry into the World Trade Organization was the capstone of its economic reform program. But the road to full membership in the chief regulatory body for international trade was long and difficult; 14 years of arduous negotiations, replete with political controversy, would take place between China's initial application to join and its ultimate acceptance.

Talks directed at bringing China into the international trade system appeared to be nearing completion by the late 1980s, but then a confluence of events derailed the negotiations. The first and most obvious of these events was the Tiananmen Square massacre of June 1989, in the wake of which most Western governments imposed economic sanctions on China. No Western government was willing to send representatives to meet Chinese trade negotiators in Geneva, where the General Agreement on Tariffs and Trade (GATT), the predecessor to the World Trade Organization, was based, so negotiations came to a standstill.

Then, in 1991, the breakup of the Soviet Union—and with that, the collapse of the trading system that tied Eastern European countries closely to the Soviet Union—raised the prospect that many more developing economies would seek to join the GATT. Since the terms of China's membership increasingly were seen as a template that would apply to other developing economies, Western governments implicitly adopted a strategy of bringing China in only on relatively rigorous terms.

By the early 1990s, China was so successful in expanding trade and in attracting foreign investment that many members of the international trade organization came to believe that China was not entitled to membership as a developing country (a status that would have automatically allowed it to enter on less demanding terms). In addition, the sheer volume of China's exports led some

Cyclists pass a bus advertising Apple iMac computers in Shanghai. With its population of approximately 1.2 billion and its growing prosperity, China presents attractive opportunities for a wide array of businesses that produce consumer goods.

governments—in both industrialized and developing nations—to regard China as a potentially serious new competitor.

The main reservations that the WTO (which officially began operating in 1995) had regarding China's application for membership centered on how well China would protect intellectual property, and on whether China would lower barriers designed to keep out foreign financial-services companies and agricultural imports. Ultimately, when China became a full member of the WTO in 2001, it was under terms that hewed closely to the long-term Western goal of bringing China into the world trading system. China promised not only to substantially reduce barriers—in the form of taxation and in the form of legal restrictions—but also to open up to foreign investment long-guarded domestic sectors such as banking, insurance, and telecommunications. Equally significant, China agreed to abide by all WTO rules such as the protection of foreign intellectual property.

The U.S. government played a significant role in tipping the scales in favor of China's admission into the WTO. In November 1999 the United States and China concluded a major bilateral trade agreement. American proponents of bringing China into the WTO touted the potential benefits to the United States. In a 2000 speech, President Bill Clinton described it as an opportunity that comes along once in a generation. That assessment was based largely on China's huge—and still largely untapped—consumer market. For example, in the year 2000, more than 35.6 million subscribers signed up for land-based telephone service; for cellular phones, the market was even greater, with 42 million new subscribers. Critics countered that China remained essentially a state-controlled economy that would not—indeed, could not—live up to its WTO commitments. (That criticism continues to be heard today. For example, foreign investors in the banking industry are still waiting for the government to hasten the pace at which it allows them to operate independent

Practitioners of Falun Gong protest the Chinese government's detention of members of their spiritual movement. During the 1980s and 1990s, some Westerners advocated withholding normal trade relations with China as a means of pressuring the government to improve its human rights record, but in the end economic considerations won out.

businesses in China rather than relying on partnerships with local businesses; the same concern applies for automakers.) In addition, critics—many of them in the U.S. Congress—opposed full trade relations with China because of the Chinese government's spotty human rights record. Besides the Tiananmen Square massacre, many critics objected to what they saw as China's repressive treatment of its Christian population; minority ethnic groups, especially the Tibetans; and practitioners of Falun Gong, a meditative movement the government claims is a cult. Since China's entry into the WTO, however, human rights issues have been separated from U.S.-China bilateral trade.

The United States, China, and the WTO

China's economy is so large that the expansion of economic production and trade resulting from its membership in the WTO is likely to affect the growth of global trade. No other country that has become a member in recent years has been large enough to affect global trade and production so positively. As the only major trading nation that does not have an advanced industrial economy, China will almost certainly bring a distinct perspective to international trade negotiations and exert its power on matters important to its trade.

China's membership in the WTO will not only continue to create new opportunities for China to export goods and integrate into the global economy; it also poses momentous opportunities and challenges for the United States and other countries. On a global level, much of the economic growth predicted from China's entry into the WTO has been felt in Asia because the economies there have closer trade ties with China and because Taiwan entered the WTO separately in early 2002. But even the United States and the European Union stand to benefit from faster economic growth resulting from the new influence of the Greater China region in international trade.

The United States is by far China's largest export market. One result has been an expanding trade deficit with China (meaning that China sells more products in the United States than the United States sells in China, creating an imbalance in the flow of goods and money), a source of concern for U.S. policymakers. Trade between China and the United States has grown rapidly since trade relations resumed in 1978. Bilateral trade turnover (the sum of the amount of exports and imports) grew from $1 billion in 1978 to $116 billion in 2000. But throughout the 1990s, the trade flows became increasingly imbalanced. By 2000 the U.S. trade deficit with China reached $84 billion and, for the first time on an annual basis, exceeded the U.S. trade deficit with Japan.

The growing trade imbalance is frequently cited as evidence that China's economy is still not completely open. But that argument is fundamentally flawed for several reasons. Most of the U.S. trade deficit with China actually stems from the concentration of labor-intensive manufacturing in China. In the 1980s and 1990s, as wages in countries such as Taiwan, South Korea, and Hong Kong rose and China loosened its regulations on foreign investment, Asian entrepreneurs started to move a large share of their labor-intensive production to China. Much of the goods the United States imports from China are actually produced in jointly owned or wholly foreign-owned factories.

China's membership in the WTO is not likely to fundamentally change the pattern of bilateral trade between China and the United States. But it should positively affect the growth of U.S. exports to China. The deficit, however, will likely expand as foreign firms move to China in large numbers. On the plus side, the exports of goods such as U.S. citrus fruits to China will grow impressively. Sunkist, for example, expected to sell $500 million worth of oranges, grapefruit, lemons, and other citrus fruit to China between 2000 and 2004.

The United States has a big stake in China's further domestic economic reforms and its deepening integration into the global economy. Most obviously, China's WTO membership serves U.S. economic interests. China's commitment to loosen the terms under which foreign firms can invest across different industries means that U.S. firms stand to benefit, since many of them are already very competitive globally. China's WTO commitments have increased access of U.S. firms to this market and increased the prospect that the trade relationship between the two countries will remain robust.

China's deeper integration into the global economy may make it a more constructive participant in international trade discussions. Deeper integration and acceleration of economic reforms will increase the likelihood that China can meet the expectations for

A small farmer's stand selling fruit in China. As U.S. companies gain a presence in the country, agricultural exports to China—including citrus fruits—are expected to increase.

improved living standards among its population of more than 1.2 billion. An economically failing China, by contrast, could impose heavy costs on the United States and the rest of the world.

Some scholars suggest that the United States take action to promote closer trading ties and to strengthen reforms within China. Many say the United States should drop economic sanctions that remain in place as a legacy of the Tiananmen Square massacre of 1989. Even though the sanctions are largely symbolic—for example, the U.S. policy of abstaining on decisions by the World Bank to give development loans to China—they might send the message that the United States seeks to block the emergence of China as a major economic power. The United States is also the only advanced industrial country that has no systematic technical assistance program to help the Chinese government develop the capacity to meet its WTO obligations.

China's emergence as a global economic power offers benefits and poses competitive challenges for its Asian neighbors as well as Japan, Europe, and the United States. Within a decade, China will probably surpass Japan and Germany to become the world's second largest trader. Should the United States and other developed countries fear China's emergence as an economic powerhouse? China will surely become a vocal and powerful voice at international trade negotiations, but even with rapid economic growth, broad changes in China will take time.

Already China is feeling the growing pains of a country moving forward with rapid economic reforms. The income gap between the rich and the poor, and between urban and rural areas in China, is widening. Farmers who feel marginalized by the increasing modernization of urban areas, and by the spread of industrialization into the countryside, may rise up to protest their diminishing status in the economy, as has already happened in some western provinces. The most impressive benefits—and the harshest costs—of bringing China into the international economic fold, contrary to the cries of China's cheerleaders and critics, could still be a long way off.

Chronology

1893 Mao Zedong is born to a modest farming family in central Hunan Province.

1911 After 11 attempts to revolt against the Qing dynasty, on October 10, a revolt at Wuchang touches off the defection of most provinces, which declare their independence from the Qing regime.

1912 On January 1, the Republic of China is set up at Nanjing, with Sun Yatsen, the leader of the 1911 revolution, as the acting president.

1921 The Chinese Communist Party is established in Shanghai.

1934–35 In an epic journey that will become known as the Long March, Chinese Communists retreat from their bases in Jianxi Province to Shaanxi Province in order to escape the attacking Nationalists.

1937 Japan attacks and occupies part of China, touching off eight years of fighting that ends with the defeat of Japan by the United States in World War II.

1945 With the end of World War II, the U.S.-backed Nationalist Party and the Chinese Communist Party—nominal allies during the fighting against Japan—begin a civil war for control of China.

1949 After its victory over the Nationalists, the Chinese Communist Party founds the People's Republic of China in October; the Nationalists, meanwhile, flee to Taiwan, where they establish the Republic of China.

1953–57 The First Five-Year Plan focuses on agriculture, land reforms, and industrialization to spark China's economy.

1958 Mao initiates the "Great Leap Forward," but the policies intended to accelerate economic growth in the country end in disaster by the early 1960s, with more than 20 million Chinese people losing their lives through malnutrition and famine.

1966 The Cultural Revolution, a 10-year upheaval that leaves China's economy and Chinese society in disarray, begins.

1976 Mao Zedong dies, effectively ending the Cultural Revolution.

1978 Deng Xiaoping takes over the reins of the Chinese Communist Party; over the next decade, he re-initiates the Four Modernizations—economic reforms to take place in agriculture, industry, science and technology, and defense.

1982 The first special economic zone (SEZ) is established in Shenzhen, just across the border from Hong Kong. The area was built as restricted zones where foreign firms could establish plants and house foreign personnel in international style.

1987 China first formally requests to apply for admission to the General Agreement on Tariffs and Trade (GATT), the predecessor to the World Trade Organization.

1989 On June 4, army units in tanks and armored personnel carriers roll into Beijing's Tiananmen Square and rout student protesters demanding political reform.

1992 Deng Xiaoping initiates a second wave of economic reforms, aiming at the privatization of state-owned corporations.

1993 Jiang Zemin succeeds Deng as the president of China.

1997 On February 19, Deng Xiaoping dies at the age of 92; on June 30, Hong Kong returns to China after a century of British colonial rule.

2001 China officially joins the World Trade Organization as a full member.

2002 Taiwan enters the WTO.

2003 Hu Jintao succeeds Jiang Zemin as the president of China; Wen Jiabao becomes premier of China.

Glossary

cadre—a cell of indoctrinated leaders or an individual promoting the interests of a revolutionary party.

capitalism—an economic system that permits the ownership of private property, allows individuals and companies to compete for their own economic gain, and generally lets free market forces determine the prices of goods and services.

collective—a large farm formed by the joining of many smaller landholdings and worked by many people, usually under government supervision.

communism—an ideology of equalizing the social conditions of life—specifically, a system that in theory seeks to abolish inequalities in the ownership of property and wealth, or seeks to redistribute wealth for equal use and advantage for all.

dynasty—a race or succession of rulers of the same line or family; the continued lordship of a race of rulers.

entrepreneur—someone who organizes, manages, and assumes the risks of a business.

imperialism—the policy or practice of extending the rule or authority of a nation over foreign lands, or of acquiring and holding colonies and dependencies.

industrialization—the overall change in circumstances accompanying a society's movement of population and resources from farm production to manufacturing production and associated services.

infrastructure—the system of public works and basic services needed for a society to function, such as sanitation, clean water, roads, and transportation.

intellectual property—any product of creative thinking (for example, an idea, an invention, an expression or literary creation, a business method, a chemical formula, or a computer program) that is unique, novel, and unobvious and that, in an economic sense, has value in the marketplace.

piracy—in the context of technology, the stealing of the codes that are used to write a computer program, or the illegal copying, distribution, and use of such software.

productivity—the amount of output per unit of input (labor, equipment, and capital), typically measured in the manufacturing sector by the number of hours it takes to produce a good, and in the service sector by the revenue an employee generates divided by his or her salary.

profit—the positive gain from an investment or business operation after subtracting all expenses.

proletariat—the working class, members of which must sell their labor in order to earn a living under a capitalist system.

revenue—total income for goods and services over a particular time period.

socialism—an economic system that is based on cooperation rather than competition and that utilizes centralized planning and distribution, controlled by the government.

stock exchange—a place where securities (shares of ownership in certain companies) are bought and sold.

Further Reading

Chai, Joseph C. *China: Transition to a Market Economy*. Oxford: Clarendon Press, 1997.

Chow, Gregory C. *China's Economic Transformation*. Malden, Mass.: Blackwell Publishers, 2002.

Fairbank, John. *China: A New History*. Cambridge, Mass.: Belknap Press of Harvard University Press, 1998.

Gruenwald, Paul, and Jahangir Aziz. "China and the Asian Crisis." In *China: Competing in the Global Economy*, ed. by Wanda Tseng and Markus Rodlauer. Washington, D.C.: International Monetary Fund, 2003.

Lander, Mark. "Selling Status and Cell Phones." *New York Times*, November 24, 2000.

Lardy, Nicholas R. *Integrating China into the Global Economy*. Washington D.C.: Brookings Institution Press, 2002.

Mastel, Greg. *The Rise of the Chinese Economy: The Middle Kingdom Emerges*. Armonk, N.Y.: M. E. Sharpe, 1997.

Segal, Adam. *Digital Dragon: High-Technology Enterprises in China*. Ithaca, N.Y.: Cornell University Press, 2003.

Spence, Jonathan. *Mao Zedong*. New York: Viking Press, 1999.

Woetzel, Jonathan R. *Capitalist China: Strategies for a Revolutionized Economy*. Singapore: John Wiley and Sons (Asia) Pte Ltd., 2003.

Wu, Jinglian. "China's Economic and Financial Reform." In *Financial Reform in China*, ed. by On Kit Tam. London: Routledge, 1995.

Internet Resources

http://www.cia.gov/cia/publications/factbook/geos/ch.html

The CIA World Factbook website provides a wealth of statistical information about China and its economy.

http://www.chinaonline.com/default.asp

A comprehensive website with news from all over China. The site breaks down the news by sector and region of the country, as well as by topic of interest.

http://sun.sino.uni-heidelberg.de/igcs/

A compilation of resources about China.

www.scmp.com

Online version of the *South China Morning Post,* the Greater China region's leading newspaper.

www.asia-inc.com

A magazine that deals with news from China as well as other parts of East Asia.

Index

Numbers in ***bold italics*** refer to captions.

Picture Credits

Page
12: PhotoDisc
16: Nixon Presidential Materials Staff/National Archives
18: Goh Chai Hin/AFP/Getty Images
20: Library of Congress
25: IMS Communications, Ltd.
26: Nik Wheeler/Aramco Services Company
28: National Archives
29: Library of Congress
32: Hulton Archive/Getty Images
36: IMS Communications, Ltd.
39: Art Resource
40: Corbis Images
41: Library of Congress
45: IMS Communications, Ltd.
48: IMS Communications, Ltd.
50: Carter White House Photographs Collection/National Archives
55: Nik Wheeler/Corbis
57: Chris Niedenthal/Time Life Pictures/Getty Images
60: IMS Communications, Ltd.
62: Weber/Three Lions/Getty Images
65: Mark Henley/Sinopix
69: Richard Jones/Sinopix
72: IMS Communications, Ltd.
76: Ricky Wong/Sinopix
79: Kevin Lee/Newsmakers/Getty Images
82: Mark Henley/Sinopix
85: Richard Jones/Sinopix
90: Kevin Lee/Newsmakers/Getty Images
92: Goh Chai Hin/AFP/Getty Images
94: PhotoDisc
97: Peter Parks/AFP/Getty Images
101: PhotoDisc
103: PhotoDisc
106: Mark Wilson/Getty Images
109: Mark Henley/Sinopix
111: Thomas Cheng/AFP/Getty Images
114: IMS Communications, Ltd.

Contributors

Shu Shin Luh is an experienced journalist who has written on a wide range of topics. As a technology reporter for the *Washington Post*, Ms. Luh covered the beginnings of the deregulation of the U.S. telecommunications industry. She has also won awards in the United States for her reporting on consumer rights.

After returning home to Asia, where she grew up in Taiwan and Hong Kong, Ms. Luh focused her reporting largely on business strategy and economic reform in Asian countries, writing first for the *Asian Wall Street Journal*, and later freelancing for publications such as the *South China Morning Post*, the *Washington Post*, *American Lawyer* magazine, and *Corporate Counsel* magazine. She has closely followed China's ascension to the World Trade Organization, writing feature analysis for *American Lawyer* and *Corporate Counsel*. She is also the author of *The People of China*, another book in this series.

Ms. Luh's book *Business the Sony Way: Secrets of the World's Most Innovative Electronics Giant*, published in May 2003, has been translated into Japanese and Chinese.

Ms. Luh currently resides in London.

Jianwei Wang, a native of Shanghai, received his B.A. and M.A. in international politics from Fudan University in Shanghai and his Ph.D. in political science from the University of Michigan. He is now the Eugene Katz Letter and Science Distinguished Professor and chair of the Department of Political Science at the University of Wisconsin–Stevens Point. He is also a guest professor at Fudan University in Shanghai and Zhongshan University in Guangzhou.

Professor Wang's teaching and research interests focus on Chinese foreign policy, Sino-American relations, Sino-Japanese relations, East Asia security affairs, UN peacekeeping operations, and American foreign policy. He has published extensively in these areas. His most recent publications include *Power of the Moment: America and the World After 9/11* (Xinhua Press, 2002), which he coauthored, and *Limited Adversaries: Post-Cold War Sino-American Mutual Images* (Oxford University Press, 2000).

Wang is the recipient of numerous awards and fellowships, including grants from the MacArthur Foundation, Social Science Research Council, and Ford Foundation. He has also been a frequent commentator on U.S.-China relations, the Taiwan issue, and Chinese politics for major news outlets.